D0146596

# Jerzy Kosinski

**Recent Titles in**
**Bibliographies and Indexes in American Literature**

# JERZY KOSINSKI

## An Annotated Bibliography

Gloria L. Cronin
and
Blaine H. Hall

*Bibliographies and Indexes in American Literature,*
*Number 15*

**GREENWOOD PRESS**
New York • Westport, Connecticut • London

**Library of Congress Cataloging-in-Publication Data**

Cronin, Gloria L.
    Jerzy Kosinski : an annotated bibliography / Gloria L. Cronin and
Blaine H. Hall.
      p.    cm.—(Bibliographies and indexes in American literature,
ISSN 0742-6860 ; no. 15)
    Includes index.
    ISBN 0-313-27442-8 (lib. bdg. : alk. paper)
    1. Kosinski, Jerzy N., 1933- —Bibliography.    I. Hall, Blaine
H.    II. Title.    III. Series.
Z8467.523.C76  1991
[PS3561.08]
016.813'54—dc20      91-21555

British Library Cataloguing in Publication Data is available.

Library of Congress Catalog Card Number: 91-21555
ISBN: 0-313-27442-8
ISSN: 0742-6860

First published in 1991

Greenwood Press, 88 Post Road West, Westport, CT 06881
An imprint of Greenwood Publishing Group, Inc.

Printed in the United States of America

The paper used in this book complies with the
Permanent Paper Standard issued by the National
Information Standards Organization (Z39.48-1984).

10 9 8 7 6 5 4 3 2 1

# Contents

# Acknowledgments

The authors would like to thank the Brigham Young University English Department and the Harold B. Lee Library and its Interlibrary Loan Department without whose support and technical assistance our work could not have been done. We are also grateful to student research assistants Luz Lewis, Theodore Kampus, Tessa Meyer Santiago, and Alan Sevison. Thanks go also to the bibliographers and scholars who have compiled earlier bibliographies and checklists on Kosinski, and whose work has helped us obtain some of the articles and books we have listed and annotated.

# Introduction

Born in 1933 in Lodz, Poland, to two brilliant young Polish Jews, Kosinski enjoyed only a brief and precocious childhood before being separated from his family in 1939 at the onset of the Nazi invasion of Poland. The story of his next six years spent brilliantly evading both Nazi's and Polish peasants in the villages of Eastern Poland has become part of the personal myth which prefaces almost every major and minor account of Kosinski's novels. Indeed, so powerful has this account of brutalization, starvation, beatings, rape, and attempted murder become that critics and reviewers have had a hard time moving beyond the biographically exotic element in each of the books to a qualitative assessment of their value as literature. Consequently, there has been more shocked outrage concerning their extreme content than dispassionate response to their political agendas, aesthetic qualities, and narrational strategies. As Calvin Trillin noted in "Uncivil Liberties" (1982) "Have you read the reviews of his last few books?. . .the black plague got a more respectful reception."

Yet despite critics and reviewers, Kosinski became a celebrated post-World War II American author, the recipient of numerous grants, fellowships, and writers' awards. He published nine novels, and several non-fiction works, as well as numerous reviews, essays, and lectures. He also taught for prestigious American academic institutions. At a rough estimate, over 70 million copies of his novels have been put into circulation. His novels have also been translated into more than 20 languages. Furthermore, as this bibliography indicates, there are now over 400 critical articles and reviews in print in English alone, the majority of these having been written in the last ten years. This suggests that despite all, Kosinski's place in American literary history is increasingly unignorable, if not assured.

Perhaps the chief clue to the meaning of this stormy and sharply divided reception was Kosinski's deliberate self-construction (aided by history) as pariah and reactionary in relationship to the bourgeois, liberal humanist American critical community, which by and large finds itself unsympathetic to postmodernism, anti-realism, and Kosinski's deliberately shocking account of depraved human nature, the sexually deviant, and the sado-masochistic. It is also clear from the balance of critical opinion that this literary establishment fails to appreciate not only the experimental strategies employed in the novels and the explicitly sexual content, but also the near nihilistic critique they offer of American politics and culture.

This critical trend, however, seems to have been increasingly challenged by a steadily mounting series of erudite essays showing more appreciation for experimental fiction and its typically radical subject matter. One is also forced to wonder how much denial of European Jewish holocaust experience and its human aftermath lies behind this increasingly unhappy American critical reception. There is also a strong bias in the criticism which implies that if the author has been pathologically altered by his experiences, his fiction is therefore invalid as literature.The simpler though equally discernible critical assumption operating here implies that if literature fails to produce an optimistic view of society and human nature ergo it is not literature but something else.

Kosinski is most profitably looked at in company with such writers as Barth, Pynchon, Barthleme, Coover, Sukenick, Kesey, Brautigan, Gass, Federman, and others who also share his sense of the fictionality of fiction, language as the prison house of perception, and the avant-garde as the appropriate site for the disruption of the bourgeois mentality. They also share a fascination with the media, numbers, fairy tales, marchen, fables, bestiaries, and allied folk-rooted forms.

Accordingly, the most analytical criticism comments increasingly on his use of the sado-masochistic, sexual deviance, and eroticism not as pseudo-pornography, but as part of the protagonist's attempt to escape through experiencing the limits of human experience. It also concentrates increasingly on his European philosophical heritage, cultural critiques, language theory, cinematic technique, hatred of collectives, experimentalism, moral perspectives, use of the grotesque, gothic inventiveness, fight for human rights, black humor, hatred of the media, minimalism, politics, narrative methods, language experiments, tricksterism, fascination with the formation of identity, and emphatic rejection of totalitarianism.

Despite such divided critical opinion, it would seem that Kosinski, the Holocaust survivor and Polish emigre, found his way, however controversially, to the center of the post-war American literary establishment where his reputation may rise or fall, but can no longer be ignored.

This makes it doubly tragic that on May 3, 1991, Kosinski, faced with an increasingly serious heart condition, depression, and inability to work, took his own life. By tying a plastic grocery bag around his head and immersing himself in his bathtub at his West 57th New York apartment, he achieved what he had always wanted—the absolute freedom to control the circumstances of the end of his own life. He had once told colleagues that he would never consider a lingering death that destroyed his freedom and left him a helpless burden to his wife and friends. As the *Newsweek* account of his death May 13, 1991, suggests, "he may have felt that at 57 his exit from the world he did not love was long overdue." Certainly his death was consistent with the testimony of his fiction, that this has been a violent, shocking, dehumanizing century of spiritual disintegration. Though by his own assessment he was a lesser rather than a major talent, most critics and scholars agree that Kosinski was the first writer to discover how to treat the Holocaust fictionally. *The Painted Bird* remains unsurpassed as one of the major Holocaust novels.

This bibliography lists primary and secondary sources by and about Kosinski through 1990. By intent, however, we have not included everything we have found, choosing instead to include only those items of substantive content. Undoubtedly, too, some items have eluded us, since Kosinski has been widely written about in many little-known or local publications. Some items have also been eliminated because the citations we found were incorrect, and others were left out because they were not available through national interlibrary loan sources.

We have included some foreign language publications, without annotations, but only those we found through our standard searching procedures. We did not search foreign language indexing publications or bibliographies.

The book reviews were taken primarily from nationally recognized magazines, journals, and newspapers published in major cities, but not exclusively so. Brief book notices or plot summaries generally have been omitted. With few exceptions, however, any review or article with substantive critical commentary has been listed and annotated.

As much as possible, the bibliographic citations have been verified from the source documents. However, because copies of articles from interlibrary loan often came without full bibliographic information on the source itself, we have assumed the citations's correctness when its use brought us the requested item.

In the annotations we have taken care to reflect the author's tone and choice of language. Annotations contain main ideas or summarize directions of thought, but do not attempt to paraphrase the course of the article or its argument. Some articles, of course, lend themselves better to this approach than do others. Generally, the annotations are descriptive rather than evaluative, but occasionally we have noted major articles. The length of the annotation does not necessarily reflect the item's importance.

This bibliography is divided into two main divisions: Primary Sources and Secondary Sources. In the first section we have categorized Kosinski's works as **Fiction—Novels, Fiction—Short Stories, Miscellaneous Writings,** and **Interviews.** Except for the interviews, the primary sources appear without annotations.

In listing the novels we have tried to discover and list all editions of each work, both English and foreign translations, hardbound and paperback. This listing has been compiled from the *Library of Congress National Union Catalog, Cumulative Book Index, Books in Print, Paperbound Books in Print, British Books in Print, British Museum Catalog,* and the *British National Bibliography,* with additional information from the RLIN

(Research Libraries Information Network) and OCLC (Online Computer Library Center) shared cataloging online databases. The foreign language translations show only the publishing information, not the translated titles.

Kosinski's nonfiction works originally published in magazines, newspapers, journals, and as recordings have been categorized as **Articles, Books, Recordings,** and **Reviews.** We categorized the interviews as primary sources on the basis that their main value to scholars is likely to be Kosinski's own comments and ideas rather than those of the interviewers.

The **Secondary Sources** section has been arranged under the following headings: **Bibliographies and Checklists, Books and Monographs, Biographical Sources, Criticism and Reviews,** and **Dissertations.** The books and dissertations have not been annotated.

In the absence of a published biography of Kosinski, we have included a list, with brief annotations, of the articles from a wide variety of magazines, newspapers, journals and recordings that provide information about Kosinski's life. Users should also be aware that in some instances the interviews with Kosinski also provide this kind of information as do some of the reviews and critical articles. Generally, we have included under **Biographical Sources** those items that focus primarily on Kosinski rather than on his works. The critical sources with significant biographical content can be found indexed under "biography" in the subject index.

In the **Criticism and Reviews** section, the sources have been listed in subsections devoted to each of Kosinski's novels, to his nonfiction books, and to foreign language sources. **General Articles and Chapters** includes those sources not limited to a discussion of a single work. The **Subject Index,** however, provides references to the specific works discussed in these sources.

**Dissertations** includes only those cited in the *Comprehensive Dissertation Index, Dissertation Abstracts International,* including the UMI CD-Rom version, that specifically name Kosinski or one of his works in the title or as a subject.

A word about the **Author Index.** In citing author's names we have regularized a single form for those with multiple citations where the form varied in the published sources. We have adopted the form with initials rather than full names as the standard, unless a majority of published sources showed a preference for the full name or for eliminating initials. The names of all authors are included in the index. Reviews of specific works by anonymous authors can be found in the appropriate subsection under **Criticism and Reviews** where the reviews follow the articles in a separate subsection.

Users will find the **Subject Index** a useful adjunct to the classified section on a specific work, referring them to relevant sources in the other sections of the bibliography, particularly the annotated articles under **General Articles and Chapters**. The subject terms have been selected from the source works themselves and will not always appear in the annotations. They have also been purposely limited to create a simple index, not an exhaustive concordance. Some terms, such as "theme," "character," "characterization," or "sexuality" have not been included, since they represent the critical commonplaces of Kosinski scholarship and would have unreasonably cluttered the index. Titles of secondary sources are not listed. However, the titles of all Kosinski's novels and nonfiction books are included.

The citations follow *The MLA Style Manual* (1985), and are numbered consecutively throughout the bibliography. Within each section and subsection the arrangement is alphabetical. To facilitate data entry on the word processor, we have arbitrarily eliminated all diacritics in names and titles.

We have tried hard to avoid omissions and errors, but inevitably a few may have slipped through. For this we apologize.

# Chronology

**1933**    Jerzy Nikodem Kosinski born June 18, Lodz, Poland to Micezyslaw and Elzbieta (Liniecka) Kosinski.

**1939-1945**    Assumed dead and forced to wander throughout the villages of Eastern Poland in flight from the Nazis.

**1942**    Suffers speech loss in traumatic accident.

**1945**    Located by parents in Lodz orphanage.

**1948**    Hospitalized after skiing accident which shocks him into recovery of his speech.

**1950-1956**    Ski instructor in Zakopane, Poland. Social instructor summers in Miedzyzdroje, Baltic Ocean.

**1953**    M.A. in Political Science, University of Lodz.

**1955**    M.A. in History, University of Lodz.

**1955-1957**    Associate Professor and Ph.D. candidate at Institute of Sociology and Cultural History, Polish Academy of Science, Warsaw. Research Assistant at Polish Academy of Arts and Science at Lomonosov, University of Russia. Publishes on revolutionary movements of the Nineteenth Century. Exhibits prize winning photographs in major international salons of photography.

**1957**    Escapes to United States in December.

**1958**    Publishes *Socjalogia Amerykanska: Wybor Prac.*

**1958-1960**   Awarded Ford Foundation Fellowship to do doctoral work at Colombia University. Researches the sociology of literary forms and language.

**1960**   Publishes non-fiction work, *The Future is Ours, Comrade: Conversations with the Russians* under pseudonym Joseph Novak. Meets Mary Hayward Weir in New York.

**1962**   Publishes *No Third Path* under pseudonym Joseph Novak. Father dies in Poland. Marries Mary Hayward Weir on January 11.

**1965**   Publishes *The Painted Bird* and *Notes of the Author on The Painted Bird*. Granted U.S. citizenship. Mary Weir's illness begins.

**1966**   Receives Best French Foreign Book Award for *The Painted Bird*. Meets Katherina (Kiki) von Frauenhofer, a lifetime companion.

**1967**   Guggenheim Fellow in Literature. Wesleyen University Center for Advanced Study, Professor of English.

**1967-1968**   Princeton University.

**1968**   Publishes *Steps* and *The Art of the Self: Essay A Propos Steps*. Mary Weir dies of a brain tumor.

**1968-1969**   Awarded a fellowship for Advanced Studies at Wesleyan University.

**1969**   Receives National Book Award for *Steps*. Delayed in his flight to the home of Sharon Tate on the night of August 7, the night of the Manson murders. Scenes from *Steps* were performed on the television show "Critique."

**1969-1970**   Senior Fellow, Council of Humanities, Princeton University.

**1970**   John Golden Fellowship in playwriting 1970-72. Award in Literature, National Institute of Arts and Letters and American Academy of Arts and Letters. "The Writers Dilemma" Sound Seminar Audio Tape produced. Fellow of Davenport College.

**1970-1973**  Visiting Professor of English Prose, School of Drama, Yale University. Resident Fellow, Davenport College, Yale University.

**1971**  Mother dies in Poland. Produces "Jerzy Kosinski: Selected Readings from *The Painted Bird*. Audio Cassette. Publishes *Being There*.

**1972**  "The Art of Self: Essay A Propos Steps reprinted in *Exile*. "Jerzy Kosinski on Fiction" Audio Cassette produced.

**1973**  Publishes *The Devil Tree*.

**1973-1975**  President of the American Center of P. E. N. Re-elected 1974, serving the maximum two terms allowed.

**1974**  Brith Sholom Humanitarian Freedom Award.

**1975**  Publishes *Cockpit*. Resolution honoring Jerzy Kosinski for his contribution as President of P. E. N.

**1977**  Publishes *Blind Date*. Writes a screenplay for *Being There*. Receives American Civil Liberties Award.

**1979**  Publishes *Passion Play*. Film version of *Being There*, starring Peter Sellers and Shirley MacLaine released. Wins Writers Guild of America Best Screenplay Award.

**1980**  Polonia Media Perspectives Achievement Award.

**1981**  Publishes revised edition of *The Devil Tree*. Screenplay of *Being There* wins British Academy of Film and Television Arts (BAFTA). Wins Best Screenplay of the Year Award. Acts in the film *Reds* as Bolshevik Zinoviev.

**1982**  Publishes *Pinball*. Accused of plagiarism in *The Village Voice* by Geoffrey Stokes and Eliot Fremont-Smith in an article entitled "Tainted Words." Defended by John Corry, Barbara Gelb, and Charles Kaiser.

**1988**   Publishes *The Hermit of 69th Street: The Working Papers of Norbert Koski* and short story "Chantal." Endows Bruno Schulz Prize of $60,000 for a foreign writer "underrecognized" in the United States. Returns to Poland for ten-day trip, his first since escaping to the West in 1957.

**1989**   Returns to Poland to national acclaim on the publication of *The Painted Bird*, the first Polish edition of any of his works.

**1991**   Commits suicide on May 3, aged 57, due to discouragement over failing health and inability to write.

# Primary Sources

# Fiction

## Novels

1. *Being There*. New York: Harcourt, 1971; London: Bodley Head, 1971; New York: Bantam; Toronto: Bantam, 1972, 1980; London: Pan, 1973; London: Corgi, 1980; London: Black Swan, 1983, 1987. Rpt. in *Seven Contemporary Short Novels*. Eds. Charles Clerc and Louis Leiter. 3rd ed. Glenview: Foresman, 1982.

   Translations: Paris: Flammarion, 1971; Munich: Knaur, 1971; Barcelona: Pomaire, 1973; Milan: Mondadori, 1973; Barcelona: Vergara, 1980.

2. *Blind Date*. Boston: Houghton, 1977; Book Club ed., 1977; London: Hutchinson, 1978; London, Corgi, 1978; New York: Bantam, 1978; New York: Arcade, 1989.

   Translations: Tel Aviv: Yated, 1979; Barcelona: 1979; Argentina: Pomaire, 1979; Frankfurt: Fischer, 1980; Tel Aviv: Tamuz, 1988.

3. *Cockpit*. Boston: Houghton, 1975; London: Hutchinson, 1975; New York: Bantam, 1976; London: Corgi, 1976; London: Arrow, 1982; New York: Arcade, 1989.

   Translations: Paris: Flammarion, 1976; Frankfurt: Fischer, 1978; Barcelona: Pomaire, 1978; Tel Aviv: Tamuz, 1980; Barcelona: Vergara, 1982; Milan: Longanes, 1983.

4. *The Devil Tree*. New York: Harcourt, 1973; London: Hart, 1973; New York: Bantam, 1974; London: Panther, 1975; Rev. and expanded ed. New York: St. Martins, 1981; Rev. and expanded ed. New York: Bantam, 1981; Rev. and expanded ed. London: Arrow, 1982; Rev. and expanded ed. New York: Seaver, 1988.

   Translations: Paris: Flammarion, 1974; Barcelona: Pomaire, 1976; Tel Aviv: Tamuz, 1980; Barcelona: Vergara, 1981; Rev. and expanded ed. Paris: Hachette, 1981.

5.  *The Hermit of 69th Street: The Working Papers of Norbert Kosky*. New
    York: Seaver, 1988.

6.  *The Painted Bird*. Boston: Houghton, 1965; London: Allen, 1966;
    Toronto: Allen, 1966; New York: Pocket, 1966, 1971; London: Corgi,
    1967; New York: Modern Library, 1970; New York: Bantam, 1972,
    1976; Rev. ed. Boston: Houghton, 1976; London: Corgi, 1976; Rev. ed.
    New York: Bantam, 1978, 1980; London: Arrow, 1982; 2nd ed. New
    York: Random, 1983; 2nd ed. New York: Bantam, 1983. New York: 2nd
    Modern Library ed, 1983.

    Translations: Amsterdam: Bij, 1966; Bern: Scherz, 1967; Frankfurt:
    Fischer, 1968; Mexico: Grijalbo, 1968; Paris: Flammarion, 1969; Tel
    Aviv: Tamuz, 1975; Barcelona: Pomaire, 1977; [Milan]: Club degli
    Editore, 1981; Barcelona: Vergara, 1982; Warsaw: Czytelnik, 1989;.

7.  *Passion Play*. New York: St. Martins, 1979; New York: Arcade, 1979,
    1989; London: Joseph, 1980; 2nd ed. New York: Bantam: 1980; London:
    Arrow, 1972, 1982.

    Translations: Paris: Fayard, 1980.

8.  *Pinball*. New York: Bantam, 1982; London: Joseph, 1982; London:
    Arrow, 1983; Rack-size ed. New York: Bantam, 1983, 1989; New York:
    Arcade, 1989.

    Translations: Tel Aviv: Amoved, 1982; Paris: Hachette, 1982;
    Barcelona: Vergara, 1982.

9.  *Steps*. New York: Random, 1968; New York: Modern Library, 1968;
    London: Bodley Head, 1969; New York: Bantam, 1969, 1978; London:
    Corgi, 1970, 1972; New York: Modern Library, 1983; New York:
    Random, 1984; New York: Vintage, 1988.

    Translations: Paris: Flammarion, 1969; Tel Aviv: Tamuz, 1980;
    Barcelona: Vergara, 1981; Warsaw: Panstwowy Instytut wydawn, 1989.

# Short Story

10.  "Chantal." *Confrontation* 37-38 (1988): 17-22.

# Miscellaneous Writings

## Articles

11. "Against Book Censorship." *Media & Methods* Jan. 1976: 20-24.

12. "'The Banned Book' As Psychological Drug—A Parody." *Media & Methods* Jan. 1977: 18-19.

13. "Being Here." *New York* 12 May 1986: 70-72.

14. "A Brave Man, This Beatty. Brave as John Reed." *Vogue* Apr. 1982: 316-18, 379.

15. "Combining Objective Data with Subjective Attitudes." *Bulletin of the American Society of Newspaper Editors* July-Aug. 1981: 19.

16. "Dead Souls on Campus." *New York Times* 13 Oct. 1970: 45.

17. "Death in Cannes." *Esquire* Mar. 1986: 81-82.

18. "Dokumenty walki o Czlowieka: Wspomnienia Proletariatczykow." [Documents Concerning the Struggle of Man: Reminiscences of the Members of "The Proletariat"]. *Przeglad Nauk Historycznych i Spolecznych [Review of Social and Historical Sciences]* 4 (1954): 411-32. Rpt. as pamphlet by Lodzkie Towarzystwo Naukowe [Scientific Society of Lodz, Poland], 1955.

19. "How I Learned to Levitate in Water." *Life* Apr. 1984: 129-32.

20. "Is Solzhenitsyn Right?" *Time* 26 June 1978: 22.

21.  "The Lone Wolf." *American Scholar* 41.4 (1972): 513-14, 516-19.

22.  "Packaged Passion." *American Scholar* 42.1 (1973): 193-94, 196, 198-200, 202, 204.

23.  "A Passion for Polo." *Polo: Official Publication of the United States Polo Association* May 1985: 115-17, 118.

24.  "Program Rewolucji Ludowej Jakoba Jaworskiego." [The Program of the People's Revolution of Jakob Jaworski]. *Przeglad Nauk Historycznychi Spolecznych [The Review of Social and Historical Sciences]* 5 (1954): 207-36. Rpt. as pamphlet by Lodzkie Towarzystwo Naukowe [Scientific Society of Lodz, Poland], 1955.

25.  "The Reality Behind the Words." *New York Times* 3 Oct. 1971: sec. 4: 13.

26.  "Time to Spare." *New York Times* 21 May 1979: A19.

27.  "To Hold a Pen." *American Scholar* 42.4 (1973): 555-56, 558, 560, 562-64, 566-67.

28.  "TV as Babysitter." Transcript of NBC *Comment* program. 3 Sept. 1972: Rpt. as "Children of TV." *Destination Tomorrow*. Ed. Jack Carpenter. Dubuque: Brown, 1972. 327-28.

29.  "Restoring a Polish Jewish Soul." *New York Times* 22 Oct. 1988: A27.

# Books

30.  *The Art of the Self: Essay A Propos Steps*. New York: Scientia-Factum, 1968, Rpt. in *Exile* 1.1 (1972): 48-67.

     Translation: *Tijd van leven—Tijd van kunst* [The Time of Life—The Time of Art]. Amsterdam: Bezige Bij, 1970. [Includes *Notes of the Author on The Painted Bird*.].

31.  *The Future Is Ours, Comrade: Conversations with the Russians*.Garden City: Doubleday, 1960; Toronto: Doubleday, 1960; London: Bodley Head, 1960; New York: Dutton, 1964. [Written under pseudonym of Joseph Novak.].

     Translations: Bern: Scherz, 1961; Mar del Plata: Cultura Moderna, 1961; Barcelona: Noguer, 1965;.

32. *No Third Path*. Garden City: Doubleday, 1962; Toronto: Doubleday, 1962. [Written under pseudonym of Joseph Novak.].

    Translations: Bern: Scherz, 1962.

33. Notes of the Author on *The Painted Bird*. New York: Scientia-Factum, 1965; 2nd ed. New York: Scientia-Factum, 1966; 3rd ed. New York: Scientia-Factum, 1967.

    Translation: *Tijd van leven—tijd van Kunst* [The Time of Life—The Time of Art]. Amsterdam: Uitgeverij de Bezige Bij, 1970. [Includes *The Art of the Self: Essays A Propos Steps*.].

34. *Socjologia Amerykanska: Wybor Prac*. [American Sociology: Selected Works.] New York: Polski Instut Naukowy w Ameryce [Polish Inst. of Arts and Letters in America], 1958. [Edited by Kosinski].

# Recordings

35. *Jerzy Kosinski on Fiction*. Audio Cassette. North Hollywood: Center for Cassette Studies, 1972.

36. *Jerzy Kosinski: Selected Readings from The Painted Bird*. Audio Cassette. New York: Westinghouse Learning, 1971.

37. *The Writer's Dilemma*. Sound Seminar Audio Tape. New York: McGraw, 1970,

# Reviews

38. "The Secret Life of Our Times." Rev. of *New Fiction from Esquire*, ed. by Gordon Lish. *New York Times Book Review* 13 Jan. 1974: 26, 28, 30.

39. "'Seven Beauties'—A Cartoon Trying to Be a Tragedy." *New York Times* 7 Mar. 1976: B1, B15.

40. "Telling Ourselves Tales to Make It through the Night." Rev. of *The White Album* by Joan Didion. *Los Angeles Times Book Review* 27 May 1979: 1, 29.

41. "Vaclav Havel and the Politics of Hope." Rev. of *Disturbing the Peace: A Conversation with Karel Hvizdala*, by Baclav Havel. *Washington Post Book World* 1 July 1990: 3, 9.

# Interviews

42. Allen, Henry. "A Painted Bird, A Painted World." *Washington Post* 30 Aug. 1971: B1, B6.

   A reported conversation with Kosinski covering his apartment, female companion (Kiki), early life, response to early physical beatings, the contents of *The Painted Bird*, his present employment and financial circumstances, and his teaching philosophy.

43. Amory, Cleveland. "Trade Winds." *Saturday Review* 17 Apr. 1971: 16-17.

   An account of a lunch with Kosinski describing his apartment, the conversation, Kosinski's Russian grandfather, his relationship with his father, and his belief that the twentieth century has been a totalitarian century. Ends with an account of his ability to hide in his apartment without being found.

44. Baker, Russell. "The Lit'ry Life." *New York Times Magazine* 4 Apr. 1982: 22.

   A brief but amusing piece in which Kosinski discusses his writing, attitudes toward reviewers, practical jokes, and other anecdotes.

45. Blake, Jeanie. "Old Man River Lures Literary Giant to City." *Times-Picayune* 21 Oct. 1979: sec. 3: 8.

   Talks about Kosinski moving to New Orleans because he wants to live near a river and because he likes Southern authors. Reports on an interview with Kosinski in his hotel room talking about his novels, his reactions to his readers, his personal life, his views on the social conditions of America, and his sense of being "pure present tense. Neither perfect, nor past."

46. Cahill, Daniel J. "Life at a Gallop." *Washington Post Book World* 16 Sept. 1979: 10.

   Kosinski talks about his polo—the backdrop for *Passion Play*, his interest in photography, his experiences as a truck driver and its impact on his later writing, his writing debut and publishing career, his work with P.E.N., and the connection between his writing and his life.

47. Frymer, Murry. "Kosinski Raps about What Television Is Doing to Us All." *Newsday* 1 July 1971: 4A-5A, 25A.

    Kosinski comments on *Being There* as sociology, his views on television dulling minds and how to solve the problem, possible benefits of television watching, and its effects on children, politics, and elections.

48. Griffin, Patricia. "Conversation With Kosinski." *Texas Arts Journal* 1 (1978): 5-11.

    An erudite discussion of the theme of language revealed in each of the novels, Kosinski's period of muteness, his theories of language, and his attempts through language to draw the reader into conflict with the characters.

49. Gross, Martin L. "Conversation with an Author: Jerzy Kosinski." *Book Digest* Nov. 1980: 19-27.

    In this interview Kosinski discusses *Being There* as a motion picture, the character of Chance Gardiner, television as passive pursuit, the issue of self-definition, his childhood escape from the Nazis, the terror of Polish peasants for the Germans, his denial that his work is cruel, his methods of early survival, his early perceptions about communists, his hatred of totalitarianism, his self-identification as a liberal Jeffersonian, his first marriage, the influence of cultural Judaism on him, the "sentimental" reviewers of his books, the danger of American philosophical lethargy, and his personal work for human rights through P.E.N.

50. Grunwald, Lisa. "Jerzy Kosinski: Tapping into His Vision of Truth." *Vineyard Gazette* 29 July 1977: 1A-2A.

    Kosinski discusses living in two worlds, his early life, *Blind Date*, contact with people, writing process, aesthetic achievements, purpose in writing, Stalinism, using the English language, the 1960s, American culture, and the value of freedom and morality.

51. Haydn, Hiram. *Words and Faces*. New York: Harcourt, 1974. 213-22.

    Reports on a question and answer session with Kosinski, Fowles, Evan Hunter, Jerome Weidman, and Calder Willingham. All writers comment primarily on their methods of composition, outlining of a new novel, personal involvement in the writing, and the creative process.

52. Kane, John. "Jerzy Kosinski." *Yale Literature Review* 141 (1972): 12-16.

    In this "interview" consisting of quotes from his novels, Kosinski comments on the unimportance of autobiography; his views on collective behavior; the sources of his rebellion against socialism; his feelings about Warsaw; his visits to Greece, Turkey, and China; his refusal to use literary agents, and dehumanization through television.

53. Kettner, Linda. "Novelist Kosinski Tells What It's Like 'Being There.'"*Cedar Falls Record* 16 Sept. 1975: 3.

Describes Kosinski's appearance and reports the highlights of a speech entitled "Living in America: The Art of Repressed Prayers" given in 1975 on the University of Iowa campus at Cedar Falls.

54. Kisor, Henry. "One-on-One with Kosinski." *Chicago Sun-Times Book Week* 9 Sept. 1979: 11-12.

Describes his visit with Kosinski and discusses Kosinski's comments on polo, *Passion Play*, his early life, his use of biographical materials, and the audience response. Also discusses Fabian's sex drive and the making of the film of his novel *Being There*.

55. Klinkowitz, Jerome. "Jerzy Kosinski: An Interview." *Fiction International* 1 (1973): 31-48. Rpt. in *The New Fiction: Interviews with Innovative American Writers*. Joe David Bellamy. Urbana: U of Illinois P, 1974. 142-68.

In this interview Kosinski discusses his early life, his education his arrival in the U.S., his vision of literature, his mastery of and love of English, the effects of his writing on the reader, the creative process, autobiographical elements in *The Painted Bird*, the influence of television and film, and his views on the relationship between the individual and the group, and between death and the lyrical.

56. Kosinski, Jerzy N. "Exegetics." *Paris Review* 97 (1985): 93-9.

Contains a brief response to several photographs and several autobiographical anecdotes.

57. Kosinski, Jerzy N. "Our 'Predigested, Prepackaged Pop Culture'—A Novelist's View." *U.S. News & World Report* 8 Jan. 1979: 52-53.

A first-person account by Kosinski covering his opinions on such topics as why the U.S. still draws so many Eastern European emigres, the nature of American freedom, why Solzhenitsyn's criticism of the U.S. is not justified, fiction as a democratic form for conveying ideas, the "evils" of disco music and popular culture, his role as adversary novelist, literature as a vehicle for enlarging the world of emotional options, the perpetual revolution in the U.S., and how the reading of novels gives the reader vicarious practice for real life.

58. Langen, R. "Interview with Jerzy Kosinski." *Canadian Literary Review* 1 (Fall-Wint. 1982): 18-28.

Kosinski discusses his views on Canada, the influence of his Canadian readership, the state of American literary affairs, P.E.N., human rights, the true subject of his fiction, the self and being, *Steps, The Devil Tree, Passion Play, Cockpit, The Painted Bird*, Marxism, totalitarianism, professionalism, Paul Tillich, autobiography, Heschel, his powers of observation, his style, and the responses of reviewers and readers to his work.

59. Lawson, Carol. "Jerzy Kosinski." *New York Times Book Review* 21 Oct. 1979: 58.

At the time of the publication of *Passion Play* Kosinski talks about his work habits, his life style, his publishing methods, his disagreement with critics who find his works filled with violence and sex, and his finding readers outside New York more sympathetic, particularly the Midwestern reader.

60. Leaming, Barbara. "*Penthouse* Interview." *Penthouse* July 1982: 128-30, 167-71.

Gives a biographical sketch of Kosinski followed by him discussing his "pornography," sex as spiritual expression, Marquis de Sade, his interest in the human body, photographic practices, interest in transsexuals, novelistic sado-masochism, popular culture's treatment of sex, his habits of disguise, his relationship to Jack Henry Abbott, his early history, his views on the Stalinist state and the Communist Party, the making of *Reds,* and the making of the film of *Being There* with Peter Sellers.

61. Movius, Geoffrey. "A Conversation with Jerzy Kosinski." *New Boston Review* 1.3 (1975): 3-6.

Kosinski discusses his appreciation of American naturalist writers, the American political dilemma, American reluctance to examine itself, popular culture, fiction as a jolt into *realpolitik*, media-promoted heroes and power brokers, his political leanings, his character Tarden, European history, the writer as social detonator, his rewriting processes, Solzhenitsyn, his identity as marginal writer, the relationship of his photography to his writings, his love of Melville's *The Confidence Man*, British writers who have influenced him, his sense of his own audience, his avoidance of plot, and his views on Conrad.

62. Nicholls, Richard E. "His Life Has Been an Open Book, but the Books Are His Lifeblood." *Philadelphia Inquirer* 14 Apr. 1984: 1D, 6D.

A report of a conversation with Kosinski in his Manhattan apartment in which he discusses the details of his everyday life, his youth in Poland during World War II, his coming to America and mastering English, his speaking and writing about the Holocaust in graphic enough terms to make people understand, the themes of his books, his marriage, and his status as a celebrity.

63. Northouse, Cameron, and Donna Northouse. "Vanhome of the Mind: An Interview with Jerzy Kosinski." *Lone Star Book Review* Nov. 1979: 6-7, 24.

Describes Kosinski's life and cites Fabian in Passion Play as his most humanistic protagonist to date. Declares Kosinski as a superb stylist and follows with Kosinski's comments on his character Fabian, horses, polo, the grotesque, marriage, *The Painted Bird*, American culture, the writer as redemptive force, *Passion Play* as fiction, his use of sexuality, and his vision of life.

64. Nowicki, R. E. "An Interview with Jerzy Kosinski." *San Francisco Review of Books* 3.1 (1978): 10-13.

In this interview Kosinski discusses the morality of Western culture, *Blind Date*, his poetry of morbidity, sex as the most reliable open door to the human soul, his relationship to existentialism, religion as a moral model, the killings in *Blind Date*, Charles Manson and his gang, the instructive power of the "destructive" protagonist, women and homosexuals in his novels, his characters as agents of emotional release, his detractors among the critics, and his belief that his work provides a direct affront to the sentimental supermarket of the spurious *avant garde*.

65. Plimpton, George A., and Rocco Landesman. "The Art of Fiction XLVI." *Paris Review* 14.54 (1972): 183-207. Rpt. in revised form in *Writers at Work: The Paris Review Interviews*. 5th Series. Ed. George Plimpton. New York: Viking, 1981. 313-38.

Kosinski discusses growing up under a Stalinist regime, his photography, the reactions of the Polish press to his work, WWII and other traumatic realities, his views on Joseph Conrad, his choice of the U.S.A., learning English, the drafts he keeps in various bank vaults, his views on language, the writing process, his reactions to the critics, his attitudes towards his audience and the Atomic Age, and his views on pop culture and television.

66. Rosenbaum, Lorrin P. "Jerzy Kosinski: The Writer's Focus." *Index on Censorship* 5.1 (1976): 46-49.

Kosinski answers questions about the artist as recluse, troubadour, and talk show performer and comments on such issues as his P.E.N. presidency, *Cockpit*, human rights versus writing, the role of P.E.N. on behalf of writers, its specific role with imprisoned writers, his future plans, repressive regimes that destroy writers, and the war he is sure lies in our future.

67. Schapp, Dick. "Stepmother Tongue." *New York Herald Tribune Book Week* 14 Nov. 1965: 6.

    An account of his impressions of Kosinski, Kosinski's early life, the contents of *The Painted Bird*, the writing of the book, and his testing of its language with a variety of English-speaking readers.

68. Sheehy, Gail. "The Psychological Novelist as Portable Man." *Psychology Today* Dec 1977: 52, 55-56, 126, 128, 130.

    An interview in which Kosinski discusses what it is readers are terrified of in his work, the relationship of experience to art, the relationship of the individual to society, the power and use of individual incidents in the novels, his personal attitudes towards his oppressors, the freeing experience of writing in English, the purposes of fiction, the psychological life of collectives, water as a traumatic image in the novels, his own paranoia, the terror and violence in the novels, corporate life in America, Americans as victims of popular culture, and the uses of sentimentality.

69. Silverman, Art. "The Renegade Novelist Whose Life Is Stranger Than Fiction." *Berkeley Barb* 25 Nov.-1 Dec. 1977: 8-9.

    Finds Kosinski's world cruel, ironic, perverse, and oddly moral. Provides mostly a biographical sketch and then covers such issues as Kosinski's perception and world view, attitudes toward totalitarianism, cowboy iconography, New York as an enormous human factory, photography, television, P.E.N., *Blind Date*, his writing process, filming his books, the ambiguous nature of human attachments, oppressive popular culture, and the loss of identity of the American public.

70. Sohn, David. "A Nation of Videots." *Media & Methods* Apr. 1975: 24-26, 28, 30-31, 52, 54, 56-57. Rpt. in *Television: The Critical View*. Ed. Horace Newcomb. New York: Oxford UP, 1976.

    In this interview Kosinski discusses visiting 10-year-old children in a classroom full of video monitors where an attack was staged and noting their preference for seeing the screens rather than the event. Also discusses his violent dislike of television as passive entertainment, various experiments with television in the classroom, the capacity of television to neutralize violence, its inability to state its relationship to reality and the environment, his terror of solitary individuals with remote controlled TV sets turning into a nation of "videots," television as the constant companionship of distracting devices, the failure of fantasy lives, his bilingual childhood, and his refusal of Polish as his literary language of choice.

71. Spring, Michael. "Jerzy Kosinski on TV." *Literary Cavalcade* Dec. 1978: 19.

Contains some of Kosinski's thoughts on television taken from the transcript of an interview. Notes how he deplores the way TV is turning human beings into spectators of life rather than living their own lives. Reports on his comments that it offers easy rewards but offers no help for people to deal with the real problems of life: crises, failure, accident, sickness, old age, and death. He questions whether young people growing up today are prepared to face the fact that most of their TV-fed expectations of life are not going to be fulfilled because the real world has little in common with the world of TV shows.

72. Teicholz, Tom. "'Being There' and Staying There: Jerzy Kosinski." *Interview* [New York] Feb. 1980: 34-35.

Kosinski discusses horses, polo, his writing process, several of his books, horse jumping technique, several of his fictional characters, his family, and his early life in Poland.

73. Teicholz, Tom. "A Blind Date with Kosinski." *East Side Express* 2 Feb. 1978: 16-17.

Teicholz discusses his meeting with Kosinski, the author's early life, publishing history, world view, comments on *Blind Date*, writing process, moral purpose, the biographical and historical background to some of his books, audience response, and his views on the cinema.

74. Varro, Barbara. "Jerzy Kosinski." *Chicago Sun-Times* 24 Nov. 1976: 27, 45.

Describes Kosinski's nocturnal "anthropological investigations into the undersides of New York night culture." Describes the contents of *Cockpit* briefly and relates these to Kosinski's own life.

75. Wallace, Mike. "A Conversation with Jerzy Kosinski." *Egyptian Pres. Sadat & Israeli Prime Min. Begin: Side by Side in Jerusalem.* Sound Cassette. Vital History Cassettes 2. New York: Encyclopedia Americana/CBS News Audio Resource Library, 1977. Side B contains Kosinski interview recorded on 28 Nov. 1977 in New York City.

76. Warga, Wayne. "Jerzy Kosinski Collides with Pop Culture." *Miami Herald* 26 Oct. 1976: 1D, 3D.

In this report of a Kosinski lecture at UCLA, Wargo gives Kosinski's views on the moral purposes of his fiction, his collision with the media and pop culture, and his castigation of Americans who lack imagination.

# Secondary Sources

# Bibliographies
# and Checklists

77. Greenstone, Maryann D. "Jerzy Kosinski: Chronicler of the Jewish Experience." *Studies in Bibliography and Booklore* 10 (Wint. 1971-72): 53-56.

   An early listing of 39 primary and secondary sources. Also includes a brief biography and chronology.

78. Klinkowitz, Jerome, and Daniel J. Cahill. "The Great Jerzy Kosinski Press War: A Bibliography." *Missouri Review* 6.3 (1983): 171-75.

   A selected list of regional press articles, mostly from 1982, dealing with the authorship controversy that the authors feel has escalated into "matters of cultural style, international politics, and journalistic ethics."

79. Nadel, Ira Bruce. "Jerzy Kosinski [Joseph Novak], 1933-." *Jewish Writers of North America: A Guide to Information Sources.* Ira Bruce Nadel. American Studies Information Guide Series 8. Detroit: Gale, 1981. 241-43.

   A listing of 33 primary and secondary sources, including bibliographies, interviews, criticism, and primary fiction and prose to 1979.

80. Rusch, Frederic E. "Jerzy Kosinski: A Checklist." *Bulletin of Bibliography and Magazine Notes* 31.1 (1974): 6-9.

   A listing of primary and secondary works by and about Kosinski through March 1973.

81. Walsh, Thomas P., and Cameron Northouse. *John Barth, Jerzy Kosinski, and Thomas Pynchon: A Reference Guide.* A Reference Publication in Literature. Boston: Hall, 1977. 55-89.

   A listing of books and articles by Kosinski to 1973 and an annotated chronological listing by year of writings about him from 1960-1973.

# Books and Monographs

82. Everman, Welch D. *Jerzy Kosinski: The Literature of Violation*. Milford Popular Writers of Today 47. San Bernardino: Borgo, 1989.

83. Lavers, Norman. *Jerzy Kosinski*. Twayne's United States Authors Series 419. Boston: Twayne, 1982.

84. Lilly, Paul R. *Words in Search of Victims: The Achievement of Jerzy Kosinski*. Kent: Kent State UP, 1988.

85. Lupack, Barbara Tepe. *Plays of Passion, Games of Chance: Jerzy Kosinski and His Fiction*. Rhodes-Fullbright International Library. Bristol: Hall, 1988.

86. Sherwin, Byron L. *Jerzy Kosinski: Literary Alarmclock*. Chicago: Cabala, 1981.

87. Tiefenthaler, Sepp L. *Jerzy Kosinski: eine Einfuhrung in sein Werk*. Abhandlungen zur Kunts-, Musik- und Literaturwissenschaft 305. Bonn: Bouvier, 1980. A revision of his doctoral dissertation at the University of Innsbruck, 1978.

# Biographical Sources

88. Brenner, Marie. "Social Stamina." *New York* 22 June 1981: 26-29.

   In an article about the social life of several writers, describes the night-time activities of Kosinski, who roams around New York streets disguised to observe the life most others know little about. "Social life is just a propellant for my main event, which is my work," he comments.

89. Chambers, Andrea. "Pages." *People Weekly* 17 Sept. 1979: 44, 48, 51.

   A biographical article of Kosinski's gypsy lifestyle, personal experience of some of what he writes, marriage and loss of his wife, his obsessions, and his destructive powers.

90. Cross, Linda. "Kosinski on Skiing." *Skiing* Nov. 1977: 143-44, 236.

   Describes Kosinski's use of skiing in *Cockpit*. Comments on the relationship between his early life, skiing experience, philosophy of skiing, and activities as a ski instructor. Also discusses his home in Crans, Switzerland. Concludes with a brief account of *Blind Date*.

91. Diehl, Digby. "Author's Put-on in a No-Death Land." *Chicago Sun-Times Showcase* 13 June 1971: 11.

   Describes Kosinski's famous joke at Yale about getting rid of too many students by suggesting killing one. Reports his comments on death, television, and death in Western Civilization.

92. Gallo, William. "Jerzy Kosinski: Writing by Chance and Necessity." *Rocky Mountain News* 30 Nov. 1977: 63, 65.

   Describes the contents of *Blind Date*. Reviews Kosinski's early life, and calls him a brilliant student of bureaucracy and the collective mind. Sees him as the adversary of passive minds, consumer culture, television, and sentimentalism. Contains his comments on the philosophical meaning of the Charles Manson killings and the meaning of his title *Blind Date*.

93. Gelb, Barbara. "Being Jerzy Kosinski." *New York Times Magazine* 21 Feb. 1982: 42, 45-46, 49, 52-54, 58.

   Provides a detailed and intimate portrait of Kosinski, the Holocaust survivor.

94. "Jerzy Kosinski [Nikodem]." *Contemporary Authors.* Ed. Claire D. Kinsman. Rev. ed. Detroit: Gale, 1976. 17-20: 416-18.

   This standard reference biography provides information about his life and education, his professional career, his memberships in organizations, a bibliography of primary and secondary works, and sidelights about his career from what he and others have said about him.

95. Johns, Sally. "Jerzy Kosinski." *Dictionary of Literary Biography Yearbook: 1982.* Eds. Richard Ziegfield, Jean W. Ross, and Lynne C. Zeigler. Detroit: Gale, 1983. 169-74.

   A brief biographical essay updating the earlier *DLB* entry. Discusses Kosinski's literary reputation and fortune since 1979 and the publication of *Passion Play.* Concentrates on his rise to celebrity status on the New York scene as well as the uproar over the 1982 *The Village Voice* challenge to the authenticity of his authorship and a possible concealed relationship with the CIA. Also contains John Corry's detailed defense of the charges published in the *New York Times.* Contains photographic material from the publications involved in the debate. Discusses his most recent novel, *Pinball.*

96. Klinkowitz, Jerome. "Kosinski, Jerzy (Nikodem)." *Contemporary Novelists.* Eds. James Vinson and D. L. Kirkpatrick. 3rd ed. New York: St. Martins, 1982. 373-74.

   A standard reference biography that briefly describes and evaluates his major novels and comments on his style. Concludes that he "fastens the reader's attention to a reality our culture has otherwise found to be unimaginable—Kosinski's own measure of the writer's greatest success." Includes a bibliography of primary and secondary works, and brief resume.

97. Kopkind, Andrew. "Kosinski Redux." *Nation* 20 Nov. 1982: 516.

   Discusses the *New York Times* account of the plagiarism rumors that have periodically affected Kosinski's career and reputation.

98. "Kosinski, Jerzy (Nikodem)." *Current Biography Yearbook: 1974.* Ed. Charles Moritz. New York: Wilson, 1975. 212-15.

   A standard reference biography of Kosinski that discusses his life, his works, his literary themes, his literary accomplishments, and quotes from interviews and articles about him and by him to characterize his life, his interests, and his achievements. A good, comprehensive overview of his life.

98a. Kroll, Jack. "The Death of a Mythmaker." *Newsweek* 13 May 1991: 72.

Describes Kosinski's suicide, failing health, depression, early life, the themes of his novels, the critical reactions to his works, and his own assessment of his accomplishments as a novelist.

99. Mount, Douglas N. "Authors and Editors." *Publishers Weekly* 26 Apr. 1971: 13-16. Rpt with corrections by Kosinski in *The Author Speaks: Selected PW Interviews 1967-1976*. New York: Bowker, 1977. 88-93.

A brief overview of Kosinski's life, career, personal idiosyncracies, teaching career, individual novels, and opinions on culture, the arts, and writing.

100. Muro, Mark. "They Can't Keep Jerzy Kosinski Down." *Boston Globe* 26 June 1984: 27, 29.

Recounts lurid stories about Kosinski, describes the purported Polish disinformation campaign against him, *The Village Voice* accusation of fraudulence, his life in America, his activities as P.E.N. president, and his views on survival.

101. Mutter, John. "Kosinski Denies *Village Voice* Charges of Extensive Writing Help." *Publishers Weekly* 9 July 1982: 11, 18.

An account of the accusations and rumors which have periodically surrounded Kosinski's career, and his responses to them.

102. Northouse, Cameron. "Jerzy N. Kosinski." *American Novelists Since World War II*. Eds. Jeffrey Helterman and Richard Layman. Detroit: Gale, 1978. Vol. 2 of *Dictionary of Literary Biography*. 100 vols. to date. 1978- . 266-75.

A *DLB* entry that provides a lengthy and excellent introductory essay on Kosinski's life, career, and individual works. Also contains photographic materials, a picture of the dust jacket and a collected galley proof from *Cockpit*. Includes a complete list of his books to date and selected references.

103. "On Kosinski." *The Devil Tree*. Rev. and expanded ed. New York: Bantam, 1981. 207-11.

Describes Kosinski's life, education, escape from Europe, career as a writer, writing, and lifestyle as an afterword to the Bantam edition of *The Devil Tree*.

104. Rosen, Richard. "Heirs to Maxwell Perkins: Seven American Writers Tell Us What They Think about Their Editors." *Horizon* Apr. 1981: 51.

Here Kosinski describes his dealings with his publishers, whom he never contracts with in advance to do a novel. Describes how he looks for a publisher who can get the work published within three or four months, who will allow several sets of galleys, and who will keep only the hard-cover rights so he can sell the paperback rights separately. Comments on his policy of ignoring editors' suggestions for changes and wanting full artistic control over his work.

105. Schwartz, Ethan. "Kosinski's Literary Homecoming." *Washington Post* 5 Apr. 1989: D1.

Describes Kosinski's trip to Poland and the publication of The Painted Bird in Polish. Quotes Kosinski on the upcoming event and the possibility of his writing in Polish in the future.

106. Shaw, Daniel. "Pride of Poland." *New York* 3 Oct. 1988: 25.

Describes Kosinski's endowing the Bruno Schulz Prize for foreign writer's insufficiently recognized in the U.S.

106a. Stanley, Allessandra. "Jerzy Kosinski, the Writer, 57, Is Found Dead." *New York Times* 4 May 1991: 10.

Describes Kosinski's activities the night before his suicide, his growing depression from his heart condition and inability to work, and the reactions of several of his friends.

106b. Treadwell, David. "Novelist Kosinski, 57, Kills Himself in N. Y. Home." *Los Angeles Times* 4 May 1991: A23.

Describes Kosinski's death, his childhood in Poland, his experiences on coming to the U.S., his writing career, several of his novels, the critical reactions to his works, the plagiarism controversy, and the irony of his death from suffocation in a bathtub of water.

107. Warga, Wayne. "Jerzy Kosinski Reaches Down into Life and Writes." *Los Angeles Times Calendar* 22 Apr. 1973: 1, 54.

Notes the recent publication of *The Devil Tree* and recounts the familiar story of Kosinski's life in Europe and escape to the U.S. Also provides a publishing history and biographical information on his marriage to Mary Weir.

# Criticism and Reviews

## General Articles and Chapters

108. Abrams, Garry. "Jerzy Kosinski Leaves 'Em Amused, Bemused, and Confused." *Los Angeles Times* 14 Nov. 1984: sec. V: 1, 12.

    A report of audience reaction to Kosinski's public lecture sponsored by UCLA and the Streisand Center for Jewish Cultural Arts.

109. Aldridge, John W. "Charting the Abyss." *The American Novel and the Way We Live Now.* John W. Aldridge. New York: Oxford UP, 1983. 53-64.

    Sees the novels as lacking an accumulation of history and sequential time—only a series of moments suspended in space without precedent or consequence. Discusses the protagonists' use of impersonations, electronic devices, and technological stratagems—all within the landscape of the terrorist. Concludes that each novel provides an oblique look at existing moral conditions and the social system itself.

110. Anderson, Don. "The End of Humanism—A Study of Kosinski." *Quadrant* Dec. 1976: 73-77.

    Provides a biography of Kosinski and a commentary on *The Painted Bird, Being There, The Devil Tree,* and *Cockpit.* Also contains snatches of material from interviews with Kosinski.

111. Archer, John. "Living in Limbo." *Listener* 28 Mar. 1985: 16- 17.

    Provides an account of Kosinski's battle against what he calls "American videots" and the attack upon the imagination in this country in the post-McCluhan age. Shows Kosinski defending traditional literary culture against "global video-hypnotism." Refers tangentially to *Being There.*

112. Baker, John F. "Kosinski—and Beyond." *Publishers Weekly* 3 Dec. 1982: 20.

An account of Jerzy Kosinski's action against the *New York Times* and the events which led up to it.

113. Bakker, J. "Language as failed therapy: Kosinski's *The Painted Bird* and *Blind Date.*" *Dutch Quarterly Review of Anglo-American Letters* 9 (1979): 203-17.

Discusses the idea that Kosinski had to learn a new language in order to appropriate it for creative purposes given the traumas associated with his childhood language, Polish. Discusses fully the prose of the Kosinski novel from this perspective.

114. Base, Ron. "Jerzy Kosinski." *Washington Post* 21 Feb. 1982: G1, G10-G12.

Describes Kosinski's annual visits to the Dominican Republic to play polo, his unusual night stalking of the exotic and bizarre, and his interest in the sexual, the violent, and the effects of celebrity. Describes the contents of several of his novels, and reports his views on a variety of random topics. Contains useful biographical information.

115. Brown, Earl B., Jr. "Kosinski's Modern Proposal: The Problem of Satire in the Mid-Twentieth Century." *Critique* 22.2 (1980): 83-87.

Discusses *Steps* as a serious attempt to deal with the condition of modern man in the twentieth century—a condition characterized by no ordered pattern, namelessness, and searching through time. Concludes with a discussion of *Being There* as a novel in which the retracing of steps as strategy of order is explored. Praises the voice of both novels as a voice not of satire, which can no longer exist, but of horror at the modern condition.

116. Bruss, Paul. "Kosinski's Early Fiction: The Problem of Language." *Victims: Textual Strategies in Recent American Fiction.* Paul Bruss. Lewisburg: Bucknell U P, 1981. 167- 82.

Describes the early novels as minimalist in technique and layered with a meaningful syntax or hierarchy of relationships. Shows how each novel demonstrates the loss of the web of social structure and individual commitment. Shows how they also discuss the problem of language in conveying this level of human experience. Concludes that "even while watching the protagonist's pursuit of a new, radical integrity, Kosinski's readers cannot avoid the sense in which his text seems to be a radical pursuit of them" because the reader is ultimately left to define him or herself as a victim of language, if not a murderer.

117. Cahill, Daniel J. "Jerzy Kosinski: Retreat from Violence." *Twentieth Century Literature* 18.2 (1972): 121-32.

Argues that Kosinski's works, like those of Nietzsche, stand as a vivid warning to mankind of its own guilt, horror, and failure of community.

Notes that his power of symbolic absurdity and relationship to an irra-
tional universe show his protagonists trapped in a world of dissolving
meaning with few fragments to shore up their ruins.

118. Cahill, Daniel J. "Kosinski and His Critics." *North American Review*
     265.1 (1980): 66-68.

     Discusses the mixed praise and disgust of the critics for his power and
     command in contemporary fiction. Provides a brief historical overview
     of his career and reception.

119. Carter, Nancy Corson. "1970 Images of the Machine and the Garden:
     Kosinski, Crews, and Pirsig." *Soundings* 61.1 (1978): 105-22.

     Argues that Kosinski's novels suggest that a giant mechanical Hercules
     is lifting our culture like Anteus away from its source of power, the nec-
     essary ground of our ever-fecund American earth. Examines the
     symbolic and iconographic presence in the texts of the car, the television
     set, and the motorcycle. Shows how Kosinski suggests that neither
     machine nor nature alone can save us, but that somehow we must effect a
     mythic and realistic reconciliation of the two. Argues for an ironic recon-
     ciliation of the two in *Being There*.

120. Clayton, Jay. "Narrative and Theories of Desire." *Critical Inquiry* 16.1
     (1989): 33-53.

     Comments on Kosinski's novels connecting sexual desire with the most
     brutal forms of violence. Suggests that in *Passion Play* Fabian's restless-
     ness and insatiable desire for sexual variety demonstrates that desire can
     have no fixed home, is always restless and ever on the move. Concludes
     that Kosinski's recent novels lead us to ask if there is a link between the
     mobility of desire and a sadistic, ultimately misogynistic violence.
     Conducts this brief discussion in the context of an article arguing the
     relationship between narrative and structures of desire.

121. Coale, Samuel. "The Cinematic Self of Jerzy Kosinski." *Modern Fiction
     Studies* 20.3 (1974): 359-70.

     Argues that Kosinski's novels illuminate the dynamic conflict between
     individual and collective forces in our contemporary age. Shows how
     each deals with the private struggle for selfhood and the violent bleak,
     solipsistic and uncertain forces which govern our lives. Concludes that
     the cinematic self has been raped by the media.

122. Coale, Samuel. "The Quest for the Elusive Self: The Fiction of Jerzy
     Kosinski." *Critique* 14.3 (1973): 25-37.

     Claims Kosinski has engaged himself totally in projecting social parables
     and defining the contemporary self against the backdrop of modern soci-

ety. Argues that his art is pervaded by an anti-collectivist method for arriving at a definition of self and posits as the greatest horror the theft of self. Discusses several of the novels from this perspective and concludes that his genius lies in his ability to recreate an elemental sense of primitive and dark reality replete with violence and sexual images. Concludes that the contours of his imagination are stark and terrible.

123. "The Conscience of the Writer." *Publishers Weekly* 22 Mar. 1971: 26-28.

A report of a panel discussion on the conscience of the writer in which Kosinski participated. He does not refer to his works but talks about how they reflect his conscience. He also deplores the lack of reading in America and how the visual media causes us to focus our attention on externals as passive observers. Comments that he writes to improve his own condition.

124. Corry, John. "A Case History: 17 Years of Ideological Attack on a Cultural Target." *New York Times Arts & Leisure* 7 Nov. 1982: 1, 28-29.

An article describing the discrediting campaign of Stokes and Fremont-Smith against Kosinski for his editorial help, his connections with the CIA, his being armed, his false identities, and his politics. Also gives responses to the allegations from Kosinski.

125. Cunningham, Lawrence S. "The Moral Universe of Jerzy Kosinski." *America* 11 Nov. 1978: 327-29.

Reviews Kosinski's life and major works, concentrating on *The Painted Bird* as a *bildungsroman*. Reviews the contents of *Being There*, and concludes with a discussion of *Cockpit*. A very general introduction to the author and his works.

126. Evans, Christopher. "Jerzy Kosinski: Passionate Player." *Minneapolis Star Saturday Magazine* 22 Sept. 1979: 8-11.

Provides biographical information about Kosinski's life in Poland, his coming to the U.S., his interests and hobbies, his education, and his professional career. Also discusses his views on life and its relationship to his writing, his views on television as a threat to our psyches and to our ability to cope with a complex world, the ways in which his novels portray social and personal problems, and why his themes deal so heavily with sex and death. Illustrated by quotes from Kosinski and from some of his novels. Describes his fiction as taking the human body and psyche and zeroing in on it brutally, like a battering ram, that reveals all the things we keep hidden away and confronts us with the human condition. Concludes that his style and vivid language drive these images into the psyche of the reader.

127. Fischer, Mary A. "Peter Sellers' Chance of a Lifetime." *Rolling Stone* 19 Apr. 1979: 63-64.

Describes Kosinski's selling the film rights to *Being There* and reports the 1971 BBC interview in which Peter Sellers responds ecstatically to the book and the opportunity to play the role of Chance Gardiner. Describes both Seller's and Kosinski's responses to film director Hal Ashby, to the book, and to the movie.

128. Fosburgh, Lacey. "Why More Top Novelists Don't Go Hollywood." *New York Times Arts & Leisure* 21 Nov. 1976: B1, B13-14.

Discusses a variety of American novelists who have refused to allow Hollywood to make movies of their novels, including Kosinski. Recounts his weekly refusals to allow a movie of *The Painted Bird* and reports Kosinski's generally disparaging remarks about the media.

129. Friedman, Melvin J. "Dislocations of Setting and Word: Notes on American Fiction Since 1950." *Studies in American Fiction* 5.1 (1977): 79-98.

Argues that while some of Kosinski's work seems conventional and his syntax regular, the latter books are full of disruptive and fragmentary elements. Comments that abstractions replace concrete language at every turn.

130. Gladsky, Thomas S. "Jerzy Kosinski's East European Self." *Critique* 29.2 (1988): 121-32.

Catalogues the Eastern European background of Kosinski and the majority of his protagonists. Argues that his novels are parables of the deracinated self divorced from a cultural context and a native tradition, trying as it were, to protect and defend itself against threatening forces that exist in the post-war world.

131. Gordon, Andrew. "Fiction as Revenge: The Novels of Jerzy Kosinski." *Third Force Psychology and the Study of Literature.* Ed. Bernard J. Paris. Rutherford: Fairleigh Dickinson UP, 1986. 280-90.

Describes the tortuous landscape of predator, executioner, and victim in the novels. Argues that as the characters become afflicted with subterfuge, disguise, and deceit, Kosinski wreaks fictional revenge on his past. Describes the fiction as strained and vindictive, working even against the reader.

132. Green, Geoffrey. "The Nightmarish Quest of Jerzy Kosinski." *The Anxious Subject: Nightmares and Daymares in Literature and Film.* Ed. Moshe Lazar. Malibu: Undena, 1983. 51-67.

Draws parallels between Kosinski's personal life and the circumstances of his characters. Discusses his use of the picaresque form and the function of social criticism in the novels. Deals with several of the novels and demonstrates how the author re-orders reality through such devices as reintegrative memory and the conversion of psychic impulses into language. Provides a detailed account of the relationship between style in the novels and the effects of nightmare. Concludes that Kosinski himself finally becomes the object of the reader's gaze.

133.  Griffiths, Gareth. "Being there, being There: Postmodernism and Post-Colonialism: Kosinsky and Malouf." *Ariel* 20.4 (1989): 132-48.

Seeks to demonstrate the stylistic and thematic features of post-colonialism and postmodernism in relation to each other by describing Kosinski's work within this critical paradigm. Notes such features as exile, linguistic dislocation, traumatic silencing, marginalization, prejudice in cross-cultural encounters, rejection of realism, concern with ideological falsity of universal values, and the inability of modern life to authenticate itself without simultaneously revealing the "authentic" as merely reflexive and self-constructed.

134.  Hamilton, Gertrude K. "Jerzy Kosinski." *Beacham's Popular Fiction in America*. Ed. Walter Beacham. 4 vols. Washington: Beacham, 1986. 3: 775-89.

A substantial standard reference article on Kosinski that discusses his publishing history, critical reception, *The Painted Bird*, and *Steps*. Also contains a list of additional sources.

135.  Hicks, Jack. "The Romance and Terror of Jerzy Kosinski." *In the Singer's Temple: Prose Fictions of Barthelme, Gaines, Brautigan, Piercy, Kesey, and Kosinski*. Jack Hicks. Chapel Hill: U of North Carolina P, 1981. 177-267.

Argues that Kosinski suggests a being posed between two tempting but impossible alternatives, an aloneness, a detachment, and a separation of the solitary self from any form of social life. Sees this as the dialectic underlying his fictional world. A lengthy and erudite exploration of the psychic, philosophical, and artistic aspects of Kosinski's work, plus the pattern of his personal life. Discusses all of the works in detail.

136.  "Jerzy Kosinski's Seventh Novel Goes to St. Martin's." *Publishers Weekly* 9 Apr. 1979: 89.

Contains Kosinski's remarks about having *Passion Play* published by St. Martins Press. Describes contents and style of the book.

137.  Kaiser, Charles. "Friends at the Top of the Times." *Newsweek* 22 Nov. 1982: 125-26.

Discusses the friendship between A. M. Rosenthal and Arthur Gelb, two great cultural czars of the *New York Times* and the two "overkill" pieces on Kosinski that have appeared in the last nine months in the *New York Times Magazine* defending Kosinski against attacks of plagiarism. Goes on to describe the extraordinary influence of both editors.

138. Kakutani, Michiko. "The Strange Case of the Writer and the Criminal." *New York Times Book Review* 20 Sept. 1981: 1, 36-39.

Describes Kosinski's correspondence with Jack Henry Abbott in which he attacks him for using his life history as an excuse for a life of criminality. Shows Kosinski pointing to the history of his own life and those of his Holocaust survivor peers and claiming "none of us became criminals. The war taught us that society must be defended from men like you, Jack Abbott." Goes on to describe Abbott's subsequent literary success and Kosinski's response to it.

139. Karl, Frederick R. *American Fictions 1940-1980: A Comprehensive History and Critical Evaluation.* Frederick R. Karl. New York: Harper, 1983. 150-55, 405-08, 502-06, 531-32.

A book-length study that makes numerous valuable comments about each of Kosinski's novels. Contains much excellent material for beginning student and scholar alike.

140. Klinkowitz, Jerome. "Betrayed by Jerzy Kosinski." *Missouri Review* 6.3 (1983): 157-171. Rpt. in *Literary Subversions: New American Fiction and the Practice of Criticism.* Jerome Klinkowitz. Crosscurrents/Modern Critiques. 3rd Series. Carbondale: Southern Illinois U P, 1985. 127-48.

Describes his essay on Kosinski as a *samizdat*—an informal treatment prepared for friends and colleagues. Contains much personal anecdote about Kosinski, the man. Attempts to sift inconsistencies in the Kosinski biography and to outline his own experiences with him.

141. Klinkowitz, Jerome. "Jerzy Kosinski." *Literary Disruptions: The Making of a Post-Contemporary American Fiction.* Urbana: U of Illinois P, 1975. 2nd ed. 1980. 82-101.

A major chapter that provides an excellent introduction for both the scholar and beginning reader of Kosinski. Deals with biographical background, individual works, style, politics, readership response, major characters, and characteristic themes.

142. Larsen, Eric. "Kosinski Again: A Letter of Dissent." *North American Review* 265.2 (1980): 61-62.

Objects to the critical acclaim Kosinski has received (specifically to Cahill's article in the Spring 1980 issue of this journal) because, based

on his own experience under Nazi domination and the criticism of
Koning, the novels are "distorting and false," incorporating an
"'American' kind of artificiality."

143. Lavers, Norman. "Jerzy Kosinski." *Critical Survey of Long Fiction*. Ed.
     Frank N. Magill. English Language Series. 9 vols. Englewood Cliffs:
     Salem, 1983. 4: 1556-66.

     A standard reference article covering Kosinski's principal long fiction,
     other literary forms, achievements, and biography. Includes an analytical
     essay discussing theme and style of narration in several of his works
     including *The Painted Bird, Being There, Blind Date, Cockpit, Passion
     Play*, and *Pinball*. Concludes with a brief bibliography.

144. Lilly, Paul R., Jr. "Comic Strategies in the Fiction of Barthelme and
     Kosinski." *Publications of the Missouri Philological Association* 4
     (1979): 25-32.

     Describes the specific comic strategies of both writers and makes useful
     comparisons and contrasts on each.

145. Lilly, Paul R., Jr. "Jerzy Kosinski: Words in Search of Victims."
     *Critique* 22.2 (1980): 69-82.

     Claims that most of Kosinski's novels probe the relationship between
     victim and oppressor and are frequently done with conflicting languages.
     Traces his insights about the behavior of language with special concen-
     tration on the creation of counterlanguage from another language, and
     the transformation of self from vulnerability to strength, from victim to
     oppressor, by means of an act of language. Treats several of the novels.

146. Lilly, Paul R., Jr. "Vision and Violence in the Fiction of Jerzy Kosinski."
     *Literary Review* 25.3 (1982): 389-400.

     Construes writer as aggressor, reader as victim, and word as weapon in
     his fiction. Claims power, not violence, is what fascinates Kosinski.
     Suggests that all of the main characters have known powerlessness and
     victimization so that violence then becomes neither an abstraction, nor
     an isolated event, but a dynamic flow of power between two agents.
     Discusses several of the novels from this perspective.

147. Martin, Terence. "The Negative Structures of American Literature."
     *American Literature* 57.1 (1985): 1-22.

     Claims that what is negative in American negatives is not simply a formula
     for rhetorical fun and self-congratulation, but an impulse to cancel institu-
     tions and practices that have developed in society so that one might celebrate
     a genuine point of beginning—with its attendant hope and promise for the

future. After developing this thesis with regard to classic Western and American tracts, theology and literature, Martin applies it to Kosinski.

148. Morgan, Thomas B. "Writer Wronged." *Village Voice* 6 July 1982: 3.

A letter to the editor providing professional and personal testimony as to Kosinski's integrity as a writer and defending him from Stokes' and Fremont-Smith's allegations of plagiarism and fraud.

149. Nathan, Paul S. "Multiple Kosinskis." *Publishers Weekly* 30 Apr. 1973: 48.

An account of Kosinski's strategy and technique for securing excellent foreign translations of his work.

150. Olney, Austin. "'From His Hand Alone'." *Village Voice* 6 July 1982: 3.

A letter to the editor giving professional and personal testimony as to Kosinski's integrity and defending him from Stokes' and Fremont-Smith's allegations of plagiarism and fraud.

151. Packman, David. "The Kosinski Controversy." *Cross Currents: A Yearbook of Central European Culture* 3 (1984): 265-67.

Deals with the rumors and charges that Kosinski does not write his own texts. Argues that ultimately the case against Kosinski is yet a further transformation of the literary legend that Kosinski has produced and that has produced him.

152. Prendowska, Krystyna. "Jerzy Kosinski: A Literature of Contortions." *Journal of Narrative Technique* 8.1 (1978): 11-25.

Argues that Jerzy Kosinski is not a moralist, but one of the postmodern novelists passed on by Dostoevsky as Evil. Claims he rejects the Christian moral universe and refuses to sign up with affirmative traditions in which a man and his transcendence count. Suggests that Celine and Camus count as his literary antecedents. Provides a critique of each of the novels from this perspective.

153. "Revealed: The Real Authors of Jerzy Kosinski's Books." *New York* 28 Feb. 1983: 37-39.

A photographic essay supposedly depicting various emigres who helped Kosinski write his novels—but the eyes reveal that they are Kosinski himself in various disguises. A satire of those who have been charging that the novels were written by others.

154. Rhein, Phillip H. "Some Comments on the Meaning of Twentieth Century Art and Literature." *Images and Innovations: Update '70's.* Ed. Malinda R. Maxfield. Papers of the Southern Humanities Conference. Spartanburg: Center for the Humanities, Converse College, 1979. 32-42.

Provides a detailed account of the political and philosophical forces that have shaped twentieth century art and literature referring only briefly to Kosinski's work.

155. Richey, Clarence W. *"Being There* and *Dasein*: A Note on the Philosophical Presupposition Underlying the Novels of Jerzy Kosinski." *Notes on Contemporary Literature* 2.4 (1972): 13-15.

Applies Heidegger's views on *Dasein*, and *Geworfenheit* to *Steps*, *The Painted Bird*, and *Being There*.

156. Romano, Carlin. "Whose Book Is It, Anyway?" *Philadelphia Inquirer* 21 Sept. 1982: 1E, 4E.

Discusses the relationship between editors and writers in general and that between Kosinski and his editors in particular. Reports on the Stokes-Fremont-Smith allegations against him. A useful account of the scandal.

157. Ross, Chuck. "Rejected." *New West* 12 Feb. 1979: 39-42.

Describes his experiment to find out what happens to an "over-the-transom" manuscript sent to publishers, using a typed manuscript of the already-published and National Book Award winner, *Steps*. Describes how all the publishers rejected it, including the book's own publisher. Contains some brief information about Kosinski and the sales of *Steps*.

158. Russell, Charles. "Individual Voice in the Collective Discourse: Literary Innovation in Postmodern American Fiction." *SubStance* 27 (1980): 29-39.

Provides an elaborate description of post-modern literature as a philosophical phenomenon and makes passing reference to a large number of writers including Kosinski.

159. Russell, Charles. "The Vault of Language: Self-Reflective Artifice in Contemporary American Fiction." *Modern Fiction Studies* 20.3 (1974): 349-59.

Argues that contemporary fiction is grounded in the recognition that all human meaning is asserted in the face of an apparently indifferent universe; hence, the construction of a vault of language which admits of the distance between language and reality. Applies this idea to Kosinski's fear of rigid patterns of language that act to constrain the imagination.

160. Safire, William. "Suppressing Fire." *New York Times* 18 Nov. 1982: A27.

Reviews the controversy aroused by the Stokes and Fremont-Smith charges against Kosinski as a plagiarist, claiming that they stem from the liberal establishment but can be traced to a Polish Communist propagandist at the U.N., Weislaw Gornicki, who is trying to discredit the works of

Kosinski. He sees no conspiracy in all this, but only a "legion of the like-minded lashing out at any artist who flouts the conventional flouting." Considers Kosinski a "kooky genius" with a fierce iconoclastic vision.

161. Sanders, Ivan. "The Gifts of Strangeness: Alienation and Creation in Jerzy Kosinski's Fiction." *Polish Review* 19.3-4 (1974): 171-89.

Dismisses as useless the attempt to hunt autobiographically through the works of Kosinski and asserts instead that to understand his viewpoint as an alienated outsider is much more to the point. Discusses each of the novels from this perspective.

162. Schiff, Stephen. "The Kosinski Conundrum." *Vanity Fair* June 1988: 114-19, 166-70.

Provides useful biographical information on Kosinski's personal life and comments at length on the literary scandal of 1982 that left the literary world convinced Kosinski was a con man and fraud. Contains interview material not found elsewhere. Also describes the contents of the forthcoming *The Hermit of 69th Street*. Recounts the effects of the 1982 scandal on Kosinski's life and attempts to reconstruct Kosinski's relationship with editors that led to the accusations of his hiring ghost writers.

163. Schneiderman, David. "Kosinski's Friends See Red." *Village Voice* 16 Nov. 1982: 3.

A rebuttal quoting Kosinski supporters replying to the accusations about the authorship of his novels made by *The Village Voice* writers Stokes and Fremont-Smith.

164. Sloan, James P. "Literary Debunking or How to Roast Your 'Favorite' Author." Third Press Review Sept.-Oct. 1975: 10-11.

Defends Kosinski as a great writer forced to put up with the debunking of "little men." Discusses *The Devil Tree*, *The Painted Bird*, and *Steps* as victims of petty reviews. A general castigation of negative reviewers who fail to grant Kosinski status as a master writer.

165. Slung, Michelle. "The Wounding of Jerzy Kosinski." *Washington Post Book World* 11 July 1982: 15.

Provides a synopsis of the 1982 charges by Stokes and Fremont-Smith against Kosinski as sole author of his works. Provides commentary on Kosinski's responses and concludes that because of Kosinski's frequent variations on key episodes in his life, he has been established as totally unreliable.

166. Smith, Dave. "Kosinski Whodunit: Who Ghost There If Not Jerzy?" *Los Angeles Times Calendar* 1 Aug. 1982: 3-5. Rpt. as "One Interpretation of Novelist's Words." *Kansas City Star* 15 Aug. 1982: I1, I9.

Reviews the substance of the Stokes and Fremont-Smith charges against Kosinski, and his defenses. Gives details of his life in Poland and his coming to America. Examines each of the charges and tries to determine the truth by quoting Kosinski, Stokes and Fremont-Smith, publishers and editors, and others who were implicated in Kosinski's supposed deceptions. An excellent overview of the controversy that comes out on the side of Kosinski.

167. Spankie, Sarah. "Top Novelist Exorcises His Ghosts." *Times* 27 Mar. 1983: 12.

Reviews briefly the controversy of Kosinski's authorship of his works, quotes his explanations and defenses, and provides some clarifying biographical information.

168. Stokes, Geoffrey, and Eliot Fremont-Smith. "Jerzy Kosinski's Tainted Words." *Village Voice* 22 June 1982: 1, 41-43.

Challenges Kosinski's ethics of authorship, role as a writer, and personal truthfulness by attempting to expose evidence of fraud and ghost writing in his composition process. Contains a great deal of interview material with various of Kosinski's friends, employers, and editors. Also contains accounts of Kosinski's rebuttals.

169. Stone, Elizabeth. "Horatio Algers of the Nightmare." *Psychology Today* Dec 1977: 59-60, 63-64.

Argues that to read Kosinski is to invite the "pith pain" of an assault on one's nerves. Claims this is because these novels pierce the social skin and go deeper and, as such, recreate the aura of nightmare paranoia and fears of psychic petrification. Sees these as the fears of infancy and myth. Concludes that we read the novels because, rather than succumbing, the heroes become inventive, industrious survivors. Details all the psychological types of defense mounted by the protagonists.

170. Wetzsteon, Ross. "Jerzy Kosinski, Existential Cowboy." *Village Voice* 11 Aug. 1975: Back page, 37-38.

Draws a picture of Kosinski engaging in insistent evasion of personal revelation. Describes him as evading interviews and presenting extremes of human existence in challenge to our capacity for self-knowledge. Describes several of the novels, recounts numerous semi-unconnected autobiographical tidbits mixed with literary criticism. Concludes with a picture of Kosinski as brilliant, charming, and haunted.

171. Will, Frederic. "Literature and the other Arts." *Antioch Review* 41.3 (1983): 339-55.

     Briefly discusses the cinematic aspects of his early novels in the context of a discussion on the nature of the arts.

172. Ziegler, Robert E. "Identity and Anonymity in the Novels of Jerzy Kosinski." *Rocky Mountain Review of Language and Literature* 35.2 (1981): 99-109.

     Argues that articulation of the sense of self is central to these novels. Claims that in these works one consistently finds two opposing types of characters: the protagonists who deliberately make their identities obscure, and the secondary characters who link their identities to their jobs or activities and products. Discusses several of the novels from this perspective.

# Being There

173. Arlen, Gary H. "From the TV Viewer's Perspective." *Watch Magazine* Mar. 1980: 54-57.

     A discussion of the film version of *Being There*, commenting on characters, plot, Peter Sellers, Shirley McLaine, American culture, and Kosinski's views of television.

174. Bolling, Douglass. "The Precarious Self in Jerzy Kosinski's *Being There*." *Greyfriar* 16 (1975): 41-46.

     Argues that *Being There* and *The Devil Tree* present protagonists profoundly unable to locate a viable identity in the threatening terrain of contemporary American culture and society. Suggests that Kosinski's concern for the plight of the self requires his protagonists to commit themselves to a strategy of denial and selection rather than passively mirroring their society. Considers that *Being There* shows the defeat of the spirit and the collapse of the spiritual. Comments at length on Kosinski's fictional strategies and artistry.

175. Brantlinger, Patrick. "What Hath TV Wrought: McLuhan's 'Global Village' or Kosinski's 'Village Videot'?" *Media & Methods* Apr. 1978: 36-41, 89-91.

     Calls *Being There* an expression of the fears that TV is undermining literacy and hastening a cultural homogenization based on mindless consumerism. Provides both an account of the role media plays in the novel and Kosinski's comments on it outside the novel. Also draws contrasts and comparisons between McLuhan and Kosinski's views on the media.

176. Carter, Nancy Corson. "1970 Images of the Machine and the Garden: Kosinski, Crews, and Pirsig." *Soundings* 61.1 (1978): 105-22.

     A discussion of Kosinski's use of television as an icon in his social commentary. Provides a detailed discussion of *Being There* which demonstrates a strange, ironic and unsettling reconciliation between machine and garden images.

177. Gogol, John M. "Kosinski's Chance: McLuhan Age Narcissus." *Notes on Contemporary Literature* Sept. 1971: 8-10.

     Suggests that *Being There* is built on the myths of Adam, Eve, Narcissus, and Echo, given a few fascinating and bizarre twists. Traces in detail the parallels between Chance and Narcissus.

178. Gordon, Andrew. "Jerzy Kosinski's *Being There* and the 'Oral Triad'." *Notes on Contemporary Literature* 19.2 (1989): 3-5.

    Calls *Being There* a political, cultural, and psychological fable about the ways television may mediate our sense of self. Rejects the oral passivity theory of television watching as the sole truth of the matter and lists Kosinski's use of such images of narcissism, mirrors, autoeroticism, and vegetable passivity. Sees Chance as a blank screen on which others may project their innermost desires.

179. Grigsby, John L. "A Mirroring of America and Russia: Reflections of Tolstoy in Jerzy Kosinski's *Being There.*"*Notes on Contemporary Literature* Sept. 1987: 6-8.

    A brief article tracing Kosinski's literary antecedents back to Tolstoy, and more specifically to *The Death of Ivan Illyich*. Draws parallels between the two major protagonists.

180. Harmetz, Aljean. "Book by Kosinski, Film by Ashby." *New York Times* 23 Dec. 1979: B1, B19.

    Discusses Kosinski's reaction to Hal Ashby's movie version of *Being There*. Describes the movie as one gigantic metaphor about celebrity, surfaces versus substance, and the evils of television. Contains comments from Ashby about his vision of the book and his editing processes. An informative article with useful interview materials from both Ashby and Kosinski.

181. Hutchinson, James D. "The 'Invisible Man' as Anti-Hero." *Denver Quarterly* 6.1 (1971): 86-92.

    Describes *Being There* as a novel about an invisible anti- hero, a product of television without free will or choice, propelled by chance, rendered pacified victim, and suffering from human isolation and loss of authentic feeling. Details key episodes in the story and concludes that the straight, progressive, narrative technique is appropriate to both story and character.

182. Lipscomb, Elizabeth Johnson. "*Being There*." Survey of Contemporary Literature. Ed. Frank N. Magill. Rev. ed. 12 vols. Englewood Cliffs: Salem, 1977. 1: 619-23.

    A standard reference article covering principal characters, a brief biography of Kosinski, a complete account of the novel, and a brief list of reviews.

183. Lupack, Barbara Tepa. "Hit or Myth: Jerzy Kosinski's *Being There*." *New Orleans Review* 13.2 (1986): 58-68.

    Calls Chance the first truly American hero in the Kosinski canon, and yet identifies him as heir to his forbears. Provides an excellent account of the contents of the novel, its themes and techniques. Concludes that this is ultimately a cruel book because it purposefully distorts and mocks what is so dear to most of us: innocence and celebrity fused into American sainthood.

184.  Murray, Raymond B. "'That Certain Krylovian Touch'; An Insight into Jerzy Kosinski's *Being There*." *Notes on Contemporary Literature* 19.2 (1989): 6-8.

Notes that in *Being There* Kosinski seems to be employing Chance as a means of making fun of the political, business, and military intelligentsia of the modern world by having them kow tow to nothing more than a television-made personality. Describes the contents of the novel and the central protagonist.

185.  Rothschild, Herbert B., Jr. "Jerzy Kosinski's Being There: Coriolanus in Postmodern Dress." *Contemporary Literature* 29.1 (1988): 49-63.

Describes the powerful tension in Kosinski's worlds between the individual and the collective. Details how the respective protagonists portray this tension and illuminate the political themes of the novels. Relates them to Shakespeare's *Coriolanus* as people rooted in political community, shaped by patrician ethos, and hostile to changing values, yet who nevertheless are trapped by change and finally develop a contempt for plebians.

186.  Tepa, Barbara J. "Jerzy Kosinski's Polish Contexts: A Study of *Being There*." *Polish Review* 22.2 (1977): 52-61.

Describes this as the first novel having an American setting and showing the tragi-comic rise to power of an illiterate. Calls it a frightening satire on American life. Details the contents of the novel and describes all the Polish contexts for various parts of the novel.

187.  Willson, Robert F., Jr. "Being There at the End." *Literature/Film Quarterly* 9.1 (1981): 59-62.

An account of the United Artist's movie version of *Being There*. Describes casting, pace, individual scenes, the narrative line, and the ending. Complains at length that Ashby's ending, biblical and surrealistic, violates our sensibilities, seems pretentious, and would have been more successful if it had let Chance sink to the bottom of the pond.

188.  Ziegler, Robert E. "Electing the Video Self: A Note on *Being There*." *Notes on Contemporary Literature* 19.2 (1989): 2-3.

Comments on *Being There* as a satire on the interrelationship of American television and politics. Notes also his interest in demythologizing and depoliticizing language to restore its original status as a vehicle for individual, personal meaning.

# Reviews

189. Aldridge, John W. "The Fabrication of a Culture Hero." *Saturday Review* 24 Apr. 1971: 25-27. Rpt. as "Jerzy Kosinski's American Dream" in *The Devil in the Fire*. John W. Aldridge. New York: Harper, 1972. 267-73.

    Sees Kosinski as being interested, not primarily in satire and social commentary, but in philosophy. His works explore the meaning of the human condition and the relation of human values to the terms of existence of an essentially amoral and anachronistic universe. Claims he belongs in the line of classic European modernism and locates *Being There* in this strain of fiction because it is a parable, a metaphorical and analogical statement of an idea. Sees the hell depicted here as that of contemporary America raised to the level of electronic derangement and populated with creatures who see only images projected initially from the television set. Provides a thorough description of the contents of the novel.

190. Broyard, Anatole. "The High Price of Profundity." *New York Times* 21 Apr. 1971: 45.

    Suggests that the reader dutifully squints through his cardboard 3-D glasses to discover what is really going on with a novel centered on a character symbolically named Chance. Recounts the story and notes that the book is full of hidden meanings until banality is fully transformed into profundity.

191. "Chance Encounters." *Times Literary Supplement* 11 June 1971: 667

    Calls *Being There* a parable built around the oddly distorted second-hand view of reality that the mass media packages and sells as the real thing. Provides a thorough explanation of the contents of the novel and concludes by applauding its humor and cautionary character.

192. Combs, Richard. "Idiots First." *Sight and Sound* 49.3 (1980): 195.

    Compares the myth of *Being There* to that in *The Great Gatsby* and *The Magic Christian*, and describes the story as terse and elliptical. Concludes that the novel makes us realize how uninhabitable and fruitless such a world is.

193. Cooke, Michael. "Recent Fiction." *Yale Review* 61.4 (1972): 603-04.

    Calls *Being There* a slender pseudo-allegory of the way even those most comfortably exalted in the chaos—presidents, corporation executives, ambassadors and wives of the same—remain prone to the superstition that the human ethos is the goal and the instrument of all our striving. Provides a brief account of the contents of the book.

194. De Feo, Ronald. "Books." *Modern Occasions* (Fall 1971): 622-24.

Expresses puzzlement over Kosinski's reputation. Concedes that his prose and use of imagery is concise and unlabored, but argues that this does not make a great novel. Objects to the parade of horrors in previous books, and complains of the lack of a unifying thread. Describes *Being There* as a horror with its brain-damaged, illiterate protagonist, Chance. Concludes that this device has produced one of the most feeble satires in English in recent years.

195. Delany, Paul. "Chance Learns How from Television." *New York Times Book Review* 25 Apr. 1971: 7, 55.

Notes that *Being There* marks Kosinski's first commitment to an American setting. Recounts the contents of the novel and complains that though it scores a few hits, it fails to convince or to convict. Sees the book's interest in its furtherance of issues of identity, individualism, and humaneness.

196. Demos, John T. "New Kosinski Novel." *Under the Sign of Pisces: Anais Nin and Her Circle* 2 (Sum. 1971): 2-3.

Briefly describes the story and the protagonist, Chance. Finds the novel terrifying in its implications, not funny, and a MacLuhanesque nightmare.

197. Farrant, James. "Fiction." *Books and Bookmen* June 1971: 35.

Recounts the tale and considers it scarcely compelling enough to maintain interest. Discusses what might be the initial implausibility, a failure of the imagination that makes the reader see things in this way. Considers the novel neither realism nor parable because there are bits of both. Considers that at best it is reducible to a suspense story because it cannot reach the ambiguities of Ballard or the mathematical precision of a Borgesian journey into past or future.

198. Finn, James. "A Rich Parable." *New Republic* 26 June 1971: 32-33.

Calls *Being There* a significant departure from *Steps* and *The Painted Bird*. Notes that the place is American, and the genre is parable, but argues that it is not up to the standard of previous works despite its powerful vision and controlled and finished style. Concludes that Kosinski proves he can work in different styles and forms.

199. Gardner, Marilyn. "A Lifelong Nobody and a Would-be Somebody." *Christian Science Monitor* 27 May 1971: 11.

Asserts that *Being There* constitutes a major philosophical critique of American affluence and mass culture. Sees it also as a clever exploration of the current media mania and its chance effects on seemingly insignificant people.

200. Garmel, Marion Simon. "Is Mr. Kosinski's Hero a Savior with Bluff?" *National Observer* 17 May 1971: 19.

Calls *Being There* a long short story on the order of *Ethan Frome*, but lacking the grotesqueries of *The Painted Bird*. Details contents and concludes that out of its own fearfulness our culture invents a savior whose only power is bluff.

201. Glassgold, Peter. "Taking a Bad Chance." *Nation* 31 May 1971: 699-700.

Reviews Kosinski's previous novels and labels *Being There* a modern parable. Recounts the plot and concludes that Chance is a Candide in reverse, who has been designed by the author to tell us that we are passive, slack-jawed observers of second-hand experience. Accuses Kosinski of being anachronistic in such a judgment since he claims he believes American apathy vanished during the period of the New Frontier.

202. Gosling, Ray. "Current Fiction." *Times* 20 May 1971: 7.

Describes the contents of *Being There* and calls it a very funny, *avant garde* book and blessedly short. Notes that it is simple and easy to read and contains a folk hero very different from the style of heroes in the 1960s.

203. Howe, Irving. "Books: A Gathering of Good Works." *Harper's* July 1971: 88-92.

Finds the novel "not the fable or allegory that some reviewers have supposed, but something smaller, fresher, more clever." Considers it a "neat literary joke" about the dominant styles of our culture, our innocence, and the paralyzing mindlessness of TV.

204. Kennedy, William. "Who Here Doesn't Know How Good Kosinski Is?" *Look* 20 Apr. 1971: 12.

Considers the enemy in the Kosinski novel any collective that denies individuality. Notes that in *Steps* the protagonist is the sum of Western culture, "trauma perceived as the normal condition." Sees *Being There* as a more mellow and comic enterprise with a subtle polemic. Discusses Kosinski's relationships with his various publishers.

205. Klinkowitz, Jerome. "Being Here." *Falcon* 4 (1972): 122-25.

Calls Kosinski an astute observer of our national way of being and accuses *Being There* of being a well-turned practical joke, as well as a commentary on Kosinski's own media reputation. Comments on the role of television in the novel and its fine artistry.

206. Kroll, Steven. "Counter-Alger." *Washington Post Book World* 30 May 1971: 2.

Calls *Being There* a parable, a kind of perverse Horatio Alger story in
Ionesco mode. Comments on the stripped-down prose, the precise and
vivid imagery, and the wit and irony.

207. Lemon, Lee T. "Review." *Prairie Schooner* 45.4 (1972): 369.

Briefly describes the plot and notes that "perhaps by the very simplicity
of the style, Kosinski convinces his readers that the implausible is plausi-
ble." Concludes by wondering whether the protagonist's simplistic
answers to problems of inflation and the cold war really are too simple to
be believable.

208. McAleer, John J. "Fiction." *Best Sellers* 1 July 1971: 173.

Describes the plot and social commentary depicted in the novel and calls
it a spoof of the "American Dream of success."

209. Midwood, Barton. "Fiction." *Esquire* Oct. 1971: 63, 66.

Briefly describes Kosinski's background and the story of the novel.
Finds the moral timely for the age of television, but argues that the plot
summary is better than the novel. Claims it is too long, too padded with
stage props and soap opera dialogue. Concludes that this novel "is a joke
blown full of tepid air, communicating neither any sense of the ordinary
world nor of a cogently realized fantasy."

210. Morgan, Edwin. "President Chance." *Listener* 10 June 1971: 760.

Calls *Being There* a spare, witty, entertaining, and tantalizing fable about
modern society. Considers the approach cool, not naggingly controlled,
and redolent with shades of Kafka's Kosinski. Describes the contents
and concludes that a hero who is illiterate without being uncommunica-
tive, and impotent without being uptight, is a refreshing conception.

211. Pritchett, V. S. "Clowns." *New York Review of Books* 1 July 1971: 15.

Calls *Being There* a neat fable that has been given, as if by magic, the
gift of nullity. Provides a character study of Chance from this perspective. Notes that the whole novel hinges on a slight but ingenious idea
carried through in excellent prose that carries the comedy delicately from
scene to scene in what amounts to a dismissal of the joke of the
American political machine.

212. Sheppard, R. Z. "Playing It by Eye." *Time* 26 Apr. 1971: 93.

Calls *Being There* "a tantalizing knuckle ball of a book delivered with
perfectly symmetrical hops and metaphysical flutters." Details the contents and describes the character, Chance. Describes Kosinski's career
and his teaching at the Yale School of Drama.

213. Stern, Daniel. "Candide in the Electronic Age." *Life* 30 Apr. 1971: 14.

Describes *Being There* as the fable of a man who is without any of the normal ingredients we associate with civilized man. Claims he is an existential hero so reduced to essence that he becomes a metaphoric mirror for those around him.

214. Tucker, Martin. "Leading the Life of Chance." *Commonweal* 7 May 1971: 221-23.

Describes how in earlier novels the hero starts out in trauma and finds stasis, while in *Being There* the reverse order is followed. The hero starts out safe and ends up in an absurd world. Provides a good description of the novel. Concludes that this is a book about the absence of being in the modern American world.

215. Updike, John. "Bombs Made Out of Leftovers." *New Yorker* 25 Sept. 1971: 132-34.

Calls this a shrewd novel and describes its contents in detail. Complains that all this symbolic superstructure and the manipulative fun it invites rests on a realistic base less substantial than sand. Argues that Kosinski's portrait of America expresses (by comparison with Nabokov's) little but the portraitist's diffident contempt for the American political and financial establishment. Calls *Being There* a feebly pleasant, dim, and truncated television version of those old Hollywood comedies where a handsome bumpkin charms the world and makes good.

216. Wall, Stephen. "Seeing Is Believing." *Observer* 23 May 1971: 29.

Details the contents of *Being There* and comments that this is an agilely set up fable that proceeds from cunning rather than compulsion. Concludes that it might be a reflection of the uncomprehending impressions of the alien in the electronic village.

217. Wedde, Jan. "Selected Books." *London Magazine* Oct.-Nov. 1971: 150-51.

Calls *Being There* a book about an allegorical figure who cannot be made truly human. Considers this a chic fable in which Kosinski has not permitted us to take Chance to heart.

218. Wolff, Geoffrey. "The Life of Chance." *Newsweek* 26 Apr. 1971: 94, 95A.

Calls *Being There* an allegory that stalks bigger game than television, and a book with a blighted and dark vision of life and no real solution for existential breakdown. Yet notes that this book moves more tenderly than previous books and seems to spring from the sweet sadness of loss rather than from hatred.

# Blind Date

219. Bruss, Paul. *"Blind Date*: The Resurgence of Relationships." *Victims: Textual Strategies in Recent American Fiction*. Paul Bruss. Lewisburg: Bicknell UP, 1981. 214-27.

   Argues that Kosinski's earlier novels, *Steps* and *Cockpit*, lacked content, while *Blind Date* shows increasing interest in the protagonist's relationships with other "survivors" who have discovered the necessity of understanding and exploring the limits of perception and language that finally give shape to their experience. Explores Levanter's sophisticated understanding of the processes of language, and hence, relationships.

220. Cahill, Daniel J. "An Interview with Jerzy Kosinski on *Blind Date*." *Contemporary Literature* 19.2 (1978): 133-42.

   An interview on *Blind Date* discussing its exploration of values and society, its repetition of some of the motifs from earlier works, the Socratic quest, the development of the soul, the influence of Jacque Monod, the autobiographical elements, the reader's decoding, the state of popular culture, violence in modern society, the meaning of the title, the structure of the novel, time, and the randomness of life's events.

221. Elmen, Paul. "Jerzy Kosinski and the Uses of Evil." *Christian Century* 17 May 1978: 530-32.

   Lists all of Kosinski's achievements, and concludes that he is one of the most rewarded of novelists. Claims that *Blind Date* is an unpromising book, full of montages, redolent with violence and the macabre, cinematographic in technique and forever providing a series of tableaux. Resents Kosinski's formula of violence used for shocking the bourgeoisie. Concludes, "We are still paying the bill for World War II and the Holocaust. Jerzy Kosinski is the spokesman of all those who were wounded by the war, even though they escaped its bullets."

222. McCullough, David W. "Jerzy Kosinski." *People, Books, & Book People*. David W. McCullough. New York: Harmony, 1981. 99- 101.

   Discusses the element of chance at play in *Blind Date* and ties this into Kosinski's own life and philosophy of fate.

## Reviews

223. Ackroyd, Peter. "Prurience." *Spectator* 11 Feb. 1978: 20.

   Accuses the novel of name dropping, cheap romance, precious fictionalizing, and flat prose. Claims "Levanter is a creature of fantasy, and like all fantasies, he becomes quickly and irredeemably boring." Argues that all the characters are treated like the object of prurient fantasy and that the subject matter of death is the easiest merchandise for a bad writer.

224.   Broyard, Anatole. "Casual Lust, Occasional Journalism." *New York Times Book Review* 6 Nov. 1977: 14.

Provides a thorough account of the contents of the novel. Describes the book as a shocking Jeremiad with a sprawling and discontinuous panorama which ultimately disintegrates. Complains that though the prose is stoical, the characterizations are incurious, and the characters self-centered. Concludes that ultimately Kosinski's aesthetic is self-centered.

225.   Cahill, Daniel J. *New Republic* 11 Mar. 1978: 34-35.

Calls *Blind Date* a book about an encounter filled with strangeness and multiple possibilities featuring George Levanter, an adventurer in life's events. Notes that the prose is chilling and controlled, designed more to evoke feeling than human action. Concludes that Kosinski is making the point that nowhere is man's responsibility and moral duty spelled out.

226.   Cook, Carole. "Books in Brief." *Saturday Review* 12 Nov. 1977: 27.

Describes the protagonist, Levanter, as being like other of Kosinski's anti-heros, almost without personality and emotionally neutral. Claims Kosinski views man as having no moral character, and of choosing survival and cheap thrills over ideology. Concludes that his novels derive their popularity from the "public's prurient desire for continuous arousal."

227.   Desmond, J. F. *World Literature Today* 52.3 (1978): 472.

Complains that *Blind Date* is built on a simplistic, mechanistic vision and lacks both dramatic progression and depth of treatment. Notes the tedious repetition of banal scenes depicting moral bankruptcy and manipulation, violence, perversion, sexual sadism, and exploitation. Also complains that scene and character are scarcely developed.

228.   Duvall, E. S. *Atlantic* Dec. 1977: 108-09.

Suggests that Kosinski keeps us fascinated in Levanter's story by means of superbly wrought prose that glides over comedy and tragedy with equal ease. Complains that the exercise is bleak and compelling and that his sterility of vision leaves little room for compassion or warmth.

229.   Gray, Paul. "Dead End." *Time* 31 Oct. 1977: 104, 106.

Describes contents of the novel and calls it an assemblage of images filled with random violence and pessimism. Complains that this pessimism lies in ambush to tell us that life is a series of blind dates beyond human planning—a message appalling to some and too simple by half.

230. Halio, Jay L., Jr. "Violence and After." *Southern Review* 15.3 (1979): 703-04.

Describes the protagonist's unsuccessful efforts to remain free after fleeing a police state because only liberty will allow chance, all there is in life, to operate. Claims that his reluctant marriage violates this philosophy, and he is punished. Considers the novel ultimately unconvincing.

231. Hand, Judson. "Down Depravity Lane." *New York Daily News* 30 Oct. 1977: 18.

Describes *Blind Date* as a novel about a series of blind dates with random violence, wickedness, raw obscenity, and eroticism. Comments on its combination of rich, highly colored texture, tycoons, sexual gluttons, brilliant scientists, and horrifying honesty.

232. Kaysen, Xana. "Kosinski: Rapist as Moralist." *New Boston Review* (Spr. 1978): 18, 22.

Discusses *Blind Date* and several of Kosinski's other novels and notes that his works present a brutish, anarchic world told in flat tone, an emblem of the flatness of modern life. Claims that the symbolism of the books fails and that they refuse to produce the overtones that critics and reviewers work so hard to find. The prose often turns out to be a string of cliches. Fate is always disinterested. The list of victims in the cause of macho self-realization is enormous. Concludes that far from being a moralist, this writer is a misanthrope, and like most misanthropes, majors in misogyny. Finally, his books are not unbiased eyewitness accounts, but propaganda for one of mankind's most disreputable ideas—"Might is Right." Finds his books ultimately numbing and diminishing, dreary and pointless in being anti-human.

233. Klinkowitz, Jerome. "Jerzy Kosinski: Puppetmaster." *Chicago Daily News Panorama* 22 Oct. 1977: 16, 22.

Calls Kosinski a consummate storyteller and describes *Blind Date* as full of deftly strung together-events and stories from his past. Notes the correspondences between Levanter and Kosinski. Commends the book for its lessons about living, biology, human conduct, and survival.

234. Knight, Anne. "Jerzy Kosinski, Self-searcher." *Horizon* Nov. 1977: 96.

Calls *Blind Date* Kosinski's most engaging novel to date. Describes his life and his earlier novels.

235. Lemon, Lee T. "Review." *Prairie Schooner* 52.3 (1978): 305.

    Calls *Blind Date* a rewrite of *Cockpit* done in picaresque style with a narrowness unworthy of a major talent. Claims this work retains grace but chooses to limit its vision because the episodic structure does not permit sustained examination of either character or society that would help us understand our situation.

236. Leonard, John. "Death Is the Blind Date." *New York Times* 7 Nov. 1977: 33.

    Calls *Blind Date* a soulscape in which the war and the Holocaust have told us the worst about ourselves and in which every social relationship is based on a corruption of power and every sexual act combines manipulation, contempt, and brutishness. Comments that in this book full of victimization, randomness, and fatal accidents, innocence is stupidity and the outlaw self sees ethics as situational. Describes contents and concludes that if ministries of justice and mercy don't exist they must be invented, and that when Kosinski learns in his fiction to respect women, he will be a fine novelist.

237. Lustig, Arnost. "Love and Death in New Jerzy." *Washington Post Book World* 27 Nov. 1977: E3.

    Describes *Blind Date* as fullblooded, scintillating, storytelling which is fatalistic, nihilistic, existentialist, and biologic. Finds his seemingly chaotic style in keeping with his world vision. Describes the contents and literary techniques of several sections of the novel.

238. Mason, Michael. "A Sense of Achievement." *Times Literary Supplement* 10 Feb. 1978: 157.

    Argues that Kosinski is not nearly as great as people like Sartre or Borges and that critics have overvalued him. Commends him for his prose, complains that the reader is bound to the perspectives of one male protagonist, and points out the disagreeable qualities of Levanter. Concludes that precisely what is grisly and exciting to the reader of Kosinski is what makes him less than a great writer.

239. Michelson, Peter F. *American Book Review* Apr. 1978: 4-7.

    Briefly describes Kosinski's career and first novel. Considers *Blind Date* a happier story with the protagonist as the boy of *The Painted Bird* grown to a man. Describes the contents and themes of the story, objecting to the novel because it favors capitalism over socialism.

240. Paulin, Tom. "Guilty Dreams." *New Statesman* 10 Feb. 1978: 193-94.

    Calls *Blind Date* the work of a vulnerable, self-conscious fantasist. Kosinski is a dangerous dreamer and a vicious bore, who has created the world as a barren place full of murderous frustration.

241. Plummer, William. "In His Steps: The Mellowing of Jerzy Kosinski."
     *Village Voice* 31 Oct. 1977: 77-79.

     Calls Kosinski a genius at recodifying the grammar of our tainted desires.
     Describes *Blind Date* as a book in which for the first time the hero is not
     incapable of subordinating his own pleasures to those of another. Concludes,
     however, that this hero's geniality has cost him much of his own power.

242. Riley, John. "Kosinski's Banquet of Forbidden Delights." *Los Angeles
     Times Book Review* 27 Nov. 1977: 4.

     Describes *Blind Date* as a book that most easily allows readers a chance
     to experience, without guilt, a whole host of hidden pleasures. Relates
     the contents and comments that this book is a combination of Kafka,
     Celine, Camus, Malraux, and Hemingway designed to ferret out all our
     normal problems in a world of abnormal behaviors.

243. Sokolov, Raymond. "Clockwork Blue." *Newsweek* 21 Nov. 1977: 121-22.

     Argues that *Blind Date* consists of much flirting with girls in hotel
     rooms, murder, rape, extortion, romancing cripples, and prostitute
     encounters. Admires the narrative talent and yet questions Kosinski's
     expectation that the reader accept all this from a morally neutral position.
     Sees this as an elegantly concocted cheap thrill and the collusion
     between writer and reader obscene, but to the point.

244. Tepa, Barbara J. "Kosinski Takes Another Chance." *Polish Review* 23.3
     (1978): 104-08.

     Calls *Blind Date* a frightening but engrossing series of blind dates with
     chance. Details the contents and notes that in each encounter the self is
     assaulted with every kind of collectivist force, from a bureaucratic sys-
     tem to language itself. Considers the violence of the book metaphorical
     rather than gratuitous and useful in establishing the image of aloneness,
     breakdown, cognition, and absurdity. Reviews several of Kosinski's
     other books and concludes that this novel heralds a brilliant return to the
     titillating style of the earlier works. Sees it as revolting, stylistically bold,
     and the work of one of America's foremost novelists.

245. Wolff, Geoffrey. "Kosinski's Killing Ground." *New Times* 9 Dec. 1977:
     86-87.

     Reviews several of Kosinski's earlier novels and calls *Blind Date* a book
     that, like all the others, stuffs our faces in the "shit and gore" with his
     anti-rhetoric. Complains that the work becomes leaner and leaner, and
     that his invention reaches further and further for curiosities, moral
     conundrums, and simple abominations. Concludes that Kosinski's fic-
     tions shine with a black light and affect the reader with their sincerity.

# Cockpit

246. Atchity, Kenneth John. *"Cockpit." Survey of Contemporary Literature.* Ed. Frank N. Magill. 12 vols. Englewood Cliffs: Salem, 1977. 2: 1334-37.

    A standard reference article on *Cockpit* covering principal characters, critical reactions, style, allusions, and the protagonist Tarden.

247. Bruss, Paul. "Cockpit: Games and the Expansion of Perception." *Victims: Textual Strategies in Recent American Fiction.* Paul Bruss. Lewisburg: Bucknell U. P., 1981. 198-213.

    Claims that *Cockpit* focuses on the problem of establishing and maintaining a relationship in face of bewildering epistemological difficulties of the twentieth century. The tone disorients readers as well, though the attempt is the demystification of human relationships. Provides an elaborate and erudite treatment of the novel.

248. Grigsby, John L. "Jerzy Kosinski's *Cockpit*: A Twentieth Century *Gulliver's Travels?" Notes on Contemporary Literature* 19.2 (1989): 8-10.

    Quotes a seminal passage from Eliot's "Tradition and the Individual Talent," and notes that put in context, *Cockpit* is best illuminated through comparison and contrast with *Gulliver's Travels* and James Fenimore Cooper. Draws several comparisons and concludes that through the use of both figures, Kosinski is establishing kinship with two maligned writers.

249. Keshawarz, Margaret Kupcinskas. "Simas Kudirka: A Literary Symbol of Democratic Individualism in Jerzy Kosinski's *Cockpit." Lituanus* 25.4 (1979): 38-42.

    Acknowledges Kosinski's objectivity and subjectivity in depicting both Eastern Europe's and America's treatment of the individual in his novels. Details Kosinski's treatment of the theme of individual versus the collective.

250. Parks, John G. "Human Destiny and Contemporary Narrative Form." *Western Humanities Review* 38.2 (1984): 99-107.

    Presents the thesis that after WWII three great forces created the existence of protean twentieth-century man. Shows how this phenomenon is reflected in the characters of Jerzy Kosinski, whose main theme of the individual versus the collective happens to be one of these three great forces. Gives a detailed discussion of *Cockpit*.

# Reviews

251. Ayres, Adrian. "*Cockpit*: Gray, Gloomy, Grim, and Gross." *Chicago Illini* 8 Nov. 1976: 10.

    Calls *Cockpit* a grim, gross book concerned with tawdry scenes from the life of its protagonist, Tarden. Commends Kosinski for his skill as a writer, but condemns him for accounts of odd sexual practices, sadomasochistic relationships, exotic methods of killing, and lack of empathetic characters. Calls the book alternately depressing and disgusting, and finally wearing thin as an antidote to middle-class niceness.

252. Barrett, Gerald. "Montage." *Michigan Quarterly Review* 15.3 (1976): 356-59.

    Sees a relationship between *Cockpit* and Melville's *The Confidence Man*. Describes the novel as a dispassionate rendering of the human condition and the ambiguities of self.

253. Baumbach, Jonathan. "Jerzy Kosinski Working Out Past Imperfections." *New York Times Book Review* 10 Aug. 1975: 3.

    Calls*Cockpit* Kosinski's more audacious and elaborate return to the seemingly random picaresque mode of *Steps*. Concludes that this book is a collection of bizarre sado-masochistic, erotic anecdotes. Provides linking commentary on the other novels as well.

254. Crain, Jane Larkin. "New Books." *Saturday Review* 23 Aug. 1975: 45.

    Calls *Cockpit* a brutally powerful, relentlessly plotted book that one devours out of curiosity to know what could possibly come next. Concludes that reality may indeed be strange and terrible, but that it is so in ways far more subtle and lifelike than Kosinski's brilliant tricksterism reveals.

255. Deemer, Charles. "Satan's Soap Opera." *New Leader* 24 Nov. 1975: 22.

    Calls *Cockpit* a bewildering book because its narrator-confessor is too exaggerated a metaphor of man's dark side to be convincing. Refuses to believe the reality of its world of horrors. Considers this novel one for the devotee with a strong stomach, a dark mood, and a yen for literary puzzles. Concludes that in this book the cards are stacked.

256. Feinstein, Elaine. "Defectors." *New Statesman* 12 Sept. 1975: 313.

    Notes that *Cockpit* moves forward with the velocity of a thriller shedding characters with laconic indifference until incident follows incident with gratuitous horror and the velocity itself becomes unnerving.

257. Foote, Bud. "Kosinski." *National Observer* 6 Sept. 1975: 17.

Sees *Cockpit* as one dimensional as it takes an idea or quality embodied in a character and pursues it *ad absurdum*. Recounts the contents and explores the character of Tarden.

258. Fuller, Edmund. "Playing Tricks on a Sordid World." *Wall Street Journal* 6 Aug. 1975: 8.

Sees *Cockpit* as compounded of Le Carre, Marquis de Sade, and Camus. Describes Tarden's extreme alienation, characteristics, and actions. Complains that after all of this, Kosinski has no illuminations. Sees it merely as a book of disgust and revulsion with life and humanity, replete with incidental gross vulgarities, unconvincingly forced into the frame of the novel. Suggests that this book is all skill.

259. Kanfer, Stefan. "Corrupt Conquistador." *Time* 4 Aug. 1975: 63.

Describes *Cockpit* as an exploration of "the classic antimonies of rationality—and of experience that defeats reason and mocks humanity." After describing the contents of the novel the reviewer concludes: "Jerzy Kosinski's work glistens with social observation and psychological apprehension. Not since Conrad has an Eastern European found so profound a voice in the English tongue. Such relentless talent, such flashes of genius make the reader hope one day for a book that can look past retribution to see a state of grace."

260. Korn, Eric. "Alienation Effects." *Times Literary Supplement* 29 Aug. 1975: 961.

Calls Kosinski a superb and enigmatic anecdotalist, a medieval homilist updated for our times, often perverse, and always astounding. Details the contents of *Cockpit* and describes the operator as more alienated than ever, the adventures more quixotic, and the incidents more bizarre. Concludes that the prose leaves one no chance of escaping from its dense, demanding moral perplexities.

261. Kramer, Hilton. "Lonely Rituals." *Commentary* Dec. 1975: 78- 80.

Calls *Cockpit* a book with a hateful protagonist, its action splintered with anecdotes and cruel entrapments, and all this recounted with detached but undisguised erotic relish and gamey anecdotes. Concludes that it finally ignores all worldly plausibility by combining the sheerest narcissistic nonsense parading as arcane wisdom.

262. Lemon, Lee T. "Freak Show." *Prairie Schooner* 50.2 (1976): 172-73.

Describes *Cockpit* as a metaphor for modern life which ultimately fails in technique and theme despite its overall slickness. Complains that this is a document with all the fascination of a trip through a carnival freak show.

263. Lingeman, Richard R. "Fables Ending in Riddles." *New York Times* 15 Aug. 1975: 33.

     Provides a detailed account of Tarden and his escapades in *Cockpit*. Concludes that this is a harsh, enigmatic novel, a profoundly chilling vision of contemporary life at whose heart is a great coldness of indifference from which all warmth and life have fled.

264. Prescott, Peter S. "Superboy." *Newsweek* 11 Aug. 1975: 76.

     Calls *Cockpit* the implacably grim, even repellant fable of a man who tries to gain absolute control of his life and fails. Argues that it should be read as an expression of the inadmissable because it is the least tolerable of Kosinski's novels. Details the contents and concludes that some of the episodes described here are self-contained tales as good as anything he has done.

265. Ricks, Christopher. "Lost Allusions." *New York Review of Books* 27 Nov., 1975: 44-45.

     Describes the contents of *Cockpit* and complains that it does not have a heart, just a flickering sequence of fantasy-violences and outwittings deliberately eschewing any center of reassuring coherence. Calls it a reel of willed nastiness full of cold odiousness. Concludes that Tarden is not a secret agent at all; he is displaced and warned, the diseased fashionable novelistic imagination licensed to commit the cruelest irresponsibilities in the name of administering salutary shocks to the complacent liberal imagination.

266. Sanders, Ivan. *Commonweal* 29 Aug. 1975: 373-74.

     Comments that in this book Kosinski demonstrates his stature as a writer of the first order. Sees him as restrained in his evocation of evil by using minor atrocities, casual cruelties, and private aberrations while always hinting at the historical models behind them. Sees Tarden as a composite of all his previous heroes. Identifies the theme of the novel as Tarden's quest for total control of his inner and outer worlds.

# The Devil Tree

267. Cahill, Daniel J. "The Devil Tree: An Interview With Jerzy Kosinski." *North American Review* 258.1 (1973): 56-66.

Kosinski discusses the likenesses between *The Painted Tree* and this novel, the structuring devices in the book, the social predicament of the protagonist, the disregard of the reader in his works, the reader and the process of decoding, the mythical aspects of the novel, the issue of defining self, his philosophy of language, muteness and preverbal states, the failure of values, the obliteration of history and the uses of heritage, sexual violence, and the devil as contemporary society.

268. Hirschberg, Stuart. "Becoming an Object: The Function of Mirrors and Photographs in Kosinski's *The Devil Tree*." *Notes on Contemporary Literature* Mar. 1974: 14-15.

Argues that in this novel we are confronted with a series of frozen and static images. Notes that although it appears Kosinski has abandoned the reader to episodic chaos, several related motifs function as formal links between seemingly disparate elements. Here disorder disappears when the episodic construction is seen as a simulation of the qualities of mirrors and photographs.

269. Hutchinson, James D. "Authentic Existence and the Puritan Ethic." *Denver Quarterly* 7.4 (1973): 106-14.

Argues that *The Devil Tree* is a book about a protagonist who is a victim of the Puritan ethic and becomes a victimizer within the framework of the American Dream. Discusses the central symbolic constructs of the novel, Jonathan Whalen as descendant of John Calvin, Joe McCarthy, Vietnam, and the lethargy of television watching. Concludes that Whalen's entrapment in the devil tree (baobab) is a symbol of the condition of modern man.

270. Klinkowitz, Jerome. "How Fiction Survives the Seventies." *North American Review* 258.3 (1973): 69-73.

Classifies contemporary American novelists into three groups: establishmentarians represented by writers like Bellow, Updike and Malamud; established innovators such as Barth, Pynchon, Vonnegut and Kosinski; and disruptive fictionists like Katz, Federman, and Sukenick. Believes that Kosinski and Barthelme will move into group one because they demonstrate "the structural art of handling the fragments of contemporary life in a sublimely synthetic manner—in a way which will soon be termed 'organic.'" Discusses the protagonist in *The Devil Tree* as wanting to "imagine [him]self apart from the herd," but cannot "because his roots are other people's branches."

# Reviews

271. "All in the Margins." *Times Literary Supplement* 6 July 1973: 783.

    Sees the novel as staged in many fragments and told in many voices full of resonance and counterpoint. Considers the language subtle, poetic, skilled, and full of random cruelty. Details contents and style.

272. Alter, Robert. "Pulp-Fiction Style, Pop-Psychology Jargon, and a Genuinely Sadistic Imagination." *New York Times Book Review* 11 Feb. 1973: 2-3.

    Calls *The Devil Tree* the sketchy design of a fantasy that strains credulity beyond belief. Accuses the book of being unpleasantly self-indulgent and slack, as well as full of stylistic and cultural cliches. Concludes that ultimately it is derivative European modernism.

273. Anderson, Elliott. "Stepping Down into Drivel." *Chicago Tribune Book World* 4 Mar. 1973: 5.

    Calls *The Devil Tree* bizarre, unbelievable, and bad. Sees the narrative as fragmentary and moving without pattern. Concludes this is a thin, bad book.

274. Bell, Pearl K. "Sterile Diversions." *New Leader* 19 Feb. 1973: 16-17.

    Calls the novel a profoundly unforgivable work because it is a lumpy bundle of mindless blather probably written by a tape recorder or a Xerox machine. Describes the prose as so doggedly flaccid that it reduces everything to a state of trivial inertia. Concludes that this novel is a vacuous put-on that should be blamed on some wicked machine.

275. Butscher, Edward. "The American Apocalypse: Three Visions." *Carleton Miscellany* 14.1 (1973-74): 131-35.

    Argues that *The Apocalypse* strives to deal with the American Apocalypse at its Protestant core." Comments on how Jonathan Wright, a young lost soul who inherits his parent's vast fortune and their more massive discontent, makes continual efforts to come to terms with a strong death instinct and his intellectual and emotional gropings towards self-discovery. Includes a sad search for sexual identity—hence becoming a precise human analogy for the nation's current dilemma.

276. Corwin, Phillip. "Evil Without Roots." *Nation* 30 Apr. 1973: 566-68.

    Considers the central thrust of the novel to be philosophical with its pessimism being expressed in a distinctly religious overtone. Notes also the counterpointed and ironic references to God and the Devil. Comments on the underlying nihilism, atheism, and existentialism of the book and recounts its contents. Considers the book disappointing because of its superficial characters and superficial ideas from a writer of obvious talent. Concludes that ultimately we see the depiction of evil without roots or any earthly base and that Kosinski's is far too important a talent to be devoured by the grotesque and petrifying commercialism he has so ably satirized.

277. Cruttwell, Patrick, and Faith Westburg. "Fiction Chronicle." *Hudson Review* 26.2 (1973): 419.

   In this brief review of recent fiction, the authors characterize *The Devil Tree* as a fable about the problem of excessive and unearned affluence. Claims the problem with the novel is that the character himself realizes that the problem of too much money is not to be taken seriously, "but in that case what is his book really *about*? Questions whether "one can make effective satire out of something proclaimed by oneself as unreal."

278. Davies, Russell. "The Ravings of the Rich." *Observer* 24 June 1973: 33.

   Calls *The Devil Tree* a chopped-up book with flat, monotonous passages that sound like the lobotomized dronings of a psychiatrist's couch. Concludes that the book ultimately fails to distinguish itself from the already considerable mass of depression literature.

279. De Feo, Ronald. "Two Disappointments, One Disaster." *National Review* 16 Mar. 1973: 322-23.

   Complains that almost every encounter Whalen has is colored by stupidity, madness, perversion, corruption, and violence. Refuses to accept the vision of the dark side of life Kosinski presents. Considers the sex, violence, and cruelty too abstract and mechanical, as if the author had been programmed to produce it. Calls the episodes implausible, savage, and incapable of making us care. Sees Whalen as disembodied and monotonous, and the narrative fractured and shallow. Finally dismisses the pornography as merely intellectualized.

280. Edwards, Thomas R. "Jonathan, Benny, and Solitude." *New York Review of Books* 22 Mar. 1973: 29.

   Describes *The Devil Tree* stylistically and provides a detailed account of its contents.

281. Fallowell, Duncan. *Books and Bookmen* Sept. 1973: 89.

   Describes Kosinski's purpose in *The Devil Tree* as the creation of a cynical inanition from which there is no escape, a listless malaise filled with near nineties static. Admits the power of the piece and Kosinski's talent with narrative.

282. Garmel, Marion Simon. "Perfect Freedom Fails Kosinski's Searching Hero." *National Observer* 10 Mar. 1973: 23.

   Calls *The Devil Tree* a novel of ideas in which he examines man's capacity for inhumanity to himself. Calls the prose poetic and the style abstractionist. Recounts much of the contents.

283. Hislop, Alan. "Company Men." *Saturday Review of the Arts* Mar. 1973: 70-71.

Describes the prose in the novel as terse and hard-edged. Notes that the theme is the mysterious relationship between self and that which is not self. Comments on the brief, elliptical scenes, the slightly more conventional narrative structure, the sexual elements, and the head-on confrontation with modern capitalistic America. Concludes that the book is not fully integrated and finishes leaving one with a sense of unfulfilled expectations.

284. Howes, Victor. "Under the Microscope: A Novel in Bits and Pieces." *Christian Science Monitor* 25 Apr. 1973: 11.

Discusses *the Devil Tree* as a book whose ingenuity and technique might not quite add up to more than the conventional alienation formula with a twist.

285. "In Brief." *New Republic* 10 Mar. 1973: 33-34.

Describes the plot and central character of *The Devil Tree*. Concludes that the brief reminders here of the power of evocation, mystery, starkness, cruelty, and the void, appear fleetingly, flicker, and ultimately go out.

286. Kauffmann, Stanley. "A Double View." *World* 27 Feb. 1973: 42- 43, 46.

Argues that two themes dominate *The Devil Tree*, power and self-consciousness. Notes that Kosinski is originally a European mind, both Eastern European and Marxist. Describes the fragmented structure that operates like a serial narrative. Details contents and concludes that Kosinski now looks at the Western world as having reached the end of a "vast apparatus of moral discipline."

287. Kiley, John B. *Critic* May-June 1973: 80-81.

Describes the form of *The Devil Tree* as full of first person fragments which backfire technically. Concludes that the sudden shifts become annoying, and complains that the central character possesses neither charm, nor humor, nor maturity.

288. Klinkowitz, Jerome. "Insatiable Art and the Great American Quotidian." *Chicago Review* 25.1 (1973): 175-77.

Describes the novel as presenting an American character's struggle with his unique quotidian. Suggests that like other Kosinski characters, he lives a schizoid existence seeking personal meaning in a society which won't allow him to create.

289. Knight, Susan. "Poor Jonathan." *New Statesman* 13 July 1973: 56-57.

Comments that Kosinski's work reminds him of the camera work of director Miklos Jansco, endlessly and coldly circling the dream figures of his obsessions as they commit torture and violation in the hunt for some spurious emotional freedom. Calls Kosinski a moralist who works with negatives and notes that if the anonymous protagonist of *Steps*, who reaches an apotheosis of indifference as a member of an execution squad is a hero of our time, we have little left to hope for. Concludes that *The Devil Tree* is fashionable, but still an emasculated version of *Steps*.

290. Lehmann-Haupt, Christopher. "Bad by Design? Or Just Bad?" *New York Times* 13 Feb. 1973: 35.

Calls *The Devil Tree* a lethal text that spreads a poisonous effluvia throughout his nervous system. Comments on the "boring" contents and concludes that the kindest thing is that perhaps the form of the novel perfectly matches the hollowness and banality of modern America and that it commits the fallacy of imitative form. Concludes that this novel, instead of being a prognosis, ends up being a symptom, somewhat like an overdose of ether.

291. Lupack, Barbara Tepa. "New Tree, Old Roots." *Polish Review* 29.1-2 (1984): 147-53.

Discusses the expanded and revised version of *The Devil Tree* and compares it with the earlier version.

292. McAleer, John J. "Fiction." *Best Sellers* 15 Feb. 1973: 525- 26.

Finds the pure flame of Kosinski's prose in this novel a laser beam. Sees Kosinski scorning a society in which people manipulate others and are in turn manipulated. Describes Whalen's efforts to be free to discover his many selves, and sees him full of contempt for a corrupt world, finding only in the non-competitive Indians of Peru people free of the tension-brought diseases tearing at the vitals of civilization.

293. Prescott, Peter S. "The Basis of Horror." *Newsweek* 19 Feb. 1973: 85-86. Rpt. as "Kosinski's Deviltry" in *Never in Doubt: Critical Essays on American Books, 1972-1985*. Peter S. Prescott. New York: Arbor, 1986. 155-57.

Sees *The Devil Tree* as a difficult, impressive novel that develops a coherent philosophy not at all pretty or comforting and that opposes most of what we were brought up to believe. Suggests that Kosinski is arguing that the bases of true sin and horror are the theft of self and the loss of absolute freedom. Notes that in this novel sex and gratuitous violence figure largely, while the diction is plain and colorless, declarative, precise, and economical. Concludes that once his purpose is grasped, this book is overwhelming.

294. Skow, John. "Strike It Rich." *Time* 19 Feb. 1973: E5, E7.

Describes *The Devil Tree* as a fiction about a neurotic, hopeless main character who is dwelt on for 200 pages. Complains that unfortunately Kosinski observes nothing of interest in him and that the entire book hangs on a few heavy scenes that merely add to the sense of futility.

295. Stade, George. "The Realities of Fiction and the Fiction of Reality."
     *Harper's* May 1973: 90, 94.

     Describes the violence in all of Kosinski's novels to date and notes of the
     latest novel, *The Devil Tree*, that it is not worth the trouble it takes to get
     to the punch line. Suggests that its fantasy does not make good fiction
     and that Kosinski's invocation of the term "objective present" is comple-
     mentary evidence of his weak grip on the multiple unrealities that
     constitute our present world.

296. Stevick, Philip. "Voice and Vision." *Partisan Review* 41.2 (1974): 305.

     Briefly comments on and illustrates his style and narrative techniques,
     which he finds "marvelously expressive" for the purposes of this novel.
     Concludes that "its parts are better than its whole, and its voice greater
     than its vision."

297. Swindell, Larry. "Kosinski's Labyrinth Is No Funny Forest; But
     Compelling, Yes." *Philadelphia Inquirer* 18 Feb. 1973: 6H.

     Finds Kosinski, as a non-native writer of English, along with Conrad and
     Nabokov, illuminating the language more than those born to it. Finds
     every syllable supporting a rhythm that stimulates reading and the
     imagery purging any possible ambiguity. Complains, however, that the
     heart of his work is not his style, but his substance. In early works he
     showed evil as inherent in man, but the devil tree symbolizes American
     malaise. Describes the protagonist's efforts to find something tangible to
     fill his emptiness. Relates this work to his other novels, all of which
     reveal a consuming interest in dead souls.

298. Taylor, Mark. "In Brief." *Commomweal* 2 Nov. 1973: 119.

     Describes *The Devil Tree* as superficially similar to others of Kosinski's
     earlier works. Details its contents and describes the nature of its implied
     social critique.

299. Wolff, Geoffrey. "Last Brave Wish to Try Everything." *Washington Post
     Book World* 25 Mar. 1973: 3, 10.

     Describes the novel in terms of the protagonists' wish to wander and to
     experience everything. Disagrees with most reviewers that this is the
     story of a poor little rich kid, believing instead that Kosinski "barely con-
     tains his contempt for Jonathan and Karen, the protagonists. Comments
     on his style and discusses his first three novels. Concludes that this novel
     shows that "Americans have confused the accumulation of wealth with
     Election. Americans have confused liberty with license to manipulate.
     American society . . . is indeed a poor little rich boy, upside down," he
     concludes.

# The Hermit of 69th Street

300. Gladsky, Thomas S. "Jerzy Kosinski: The Polish Cooper." *Notes on Contemporary Literature* 19.2 (1989): 11-12.

Discusses the implications of Kosinski's use of a dozen quotes from James Fenimore Cooper in *The Hermit* to characterize Kosky, as well as himself, as the maligned author rejected by his native land. Finds this comparison of Kosinski to Cooper problematic because Cooper came passionately to the defense and support of Poland during its war with czarist Russia and, while he was denounced by some for his writing about the faults of Americans in comparison with Europeans, he was highly respected in America and wrote about America passionately. Suggests that Kosinski does not have this relationship with either Poland or America.

301. Hirschberg, Stuart. "A Note on an Episode in Jerzy Kosinski's *The Hermit of 69th Street*." *Notes on Contemporary Literature* 19.2 (1989): 5-6.

Provides a note on *The Hermit of 69th Street* describing his own rebuttal of charges of plagiarism leveled against Kosinski and the letters that this action drew in response. Sees this episode as the source of some of the book's episodes, namely the reference to 'Stone 1908.'

## Reviews

302. Batchelor, John Calvin. "The Annotated 'Roman a Tease.'." *New York Times Book Review* 3 July 1988: 11.

Calls the style and contents of the novel "autofiction." Describes all the characters, the details of the Kosky manuscript, and Kosky himself. Calls the whole production a poison-pen letter that will serve as an antidote to an over-examined life. Considers the writing witty and fluid.

303. Blades, John. "Jerzy Kosinski's *Hermit* Drives Critic to 'Murder'." *Chicago Tribune Books* 15 May 1988: 3.

Considers this novel a chaotic 500-page Hefty bag of quasi pornography, numerology, dirty talk, assorted mysticism, coy autobiographical scraps, puns, and unfamiliar quotations.

304. "Fiction." *Jim Kobak's Kirkus Reviews* 1 May 1988: 645-46.

Calls the novel an even deeper dead-end than the enervating *Pinball*. Complains that Kosinski buries the reader under a staggering blanket of boredom. Describes the "colorful" contents.

305. Goodman, Walter. "Jerzy Kosinski's Fiction of Parallels." *New York Times* 20 June 1988: C17.

Details the resemblances between Kosinski and his hero, Kosky, and recounts the fraud accusations both dealt with. Calls the book self-consciousness cluttered with flotsam, boldfaced quotations, and women as sexual objects. Dismisses all the intellectual trappings of the book and calls it "sex-lit chat" not likely to hold many readers.

306. McCaffery, Larry. "Kosinski's Mask Behind the Mask." *Washington Post Book World* 10 July 1988: 1, 9.

Calls *Hermit*, Kosinski's ninth novel, a peculiar blending of intimate revelations and abstract musings on the nature of self and the sources of artistic creativity. Sees it as his most ambitious, experimental, and nakedly confessional work to date. Concludes that this is an obsessively self-involved experimental work so obviously written for Kosinski himself that it seems born out of a sense of necessity and compulsion rare among writers, but common among survivors.

307. Richwine, K. N. "Language and Literature: English and American." *Choice* Dec. 1988: 646.

Calls this novel self-proclaimed "autofiction" that is full of ambiguity. Details the contents, calls it a stab at postmodern fiction because it is full of Joycean word play, sophomoric games with numbers, and too many interlarded quotes.

308. Singer, Brett. "Kosinski Minus the Sins." *Los Angeles Times Book Review* 25 Sept. 1988: 3, 12.

Discusses *The Hermit of 69th Street*, Kosinski's ninth novel, as a dizzying, mystical word and world-drunk piece of "autofiction." Lists sin and redemption, the spiritual life of the writer in exile, and the ethical desiderata of the post-holocaust Jew as among the hundreds of topics Kosinski takes on in this book. Describes him as the spiritual friend of Bruno Schulz, Nabokov, Conrad, Wolfe, and Cooper.

# The Painted Bird

309. Berman, Ronald. *"The Painted Bird." Survey of Contemporary Literature.* Rev. ed. 12 vols. Englewood Cliffs: Salem, 1977. 9: 5699-5701.

   A standard reference article on *The Painted Bird* covering principal characters, contents, style, symbolism, and chief events.

310. Cohn, Dorrit. "Fictional *versus* Historical Lives: Borderlines and Borderline Cases." *Journal of Narrative Technique* 19.1 (1989): 3-24.

   Argues that *The Painted Bird* among other pieces, condemns us to vacillate or oscillate not only between different modes of fictional readings, but also, more radically, between fictional and referential readings. A brief paragraph-length treatment in the context of a lengthy article on the relationship between history and narrative in Paul Ricoeur's *Time and Narrative* (1985).

311. Corngold, Stanley. "Jerzy Kosinski's *The Painted Bird*: Language Lost and Regained." *Mosaic* 6.4 (1973): 153-67.

   Discusses the background of the novel and provides a clear account of its contents. Describes it as fictional autobiography which touches the heart of Western poetic consciousness. Also discusses its contribution to developments in the fictional use of language. Talks of the relationship between Kosinski and Proust, and provides a very detailed treatment of the stylistic aspects of the novel and Kosinski's qualities of imagination.

312. Guerard, Albert J. "Notes on the Rhetoric of Anti-Realist Fiction." *TriQuarterly* 30 (1974): 31-36.

   This is a major article devoted to describing the actual rhetoric of the post-modern novel. Kosinski is one of many authors examined. Describes *The Painted Bird* as demonstrating the psychological process as rhetoric because of such techniques as displacement and fantasy, particularly surrounding scenes to do with the torture of animals and sexuality. Concludes that the great originality of *The Painted Bird* lies in its interweaving of real reality with fantasy-wish fulfillment where trauma is dealt with not as repression, but as liberated fantasy.

313. Hanson, John H. "The Child Archetype and Modern Primitivism: Kosinski's *The Painted Bird*." *Hartford Studies in Literature* 14.3 (1982): 85-95.

   Provides an elaborate history of the child as archetype through various ages in Western history. Sees this novel as psychologically a product both of fascist/communist terror and of fairy tale and myth, and as such, embodies a crisis of identity of psychotic proportions. Describes the story as a picaresque, infernal tale of a child's nightmare viaticum through Europe of WWII. Concludes that it portrays a total immersion in death—the ultimate violence to self—and the final solution of a mythopathic society.

314. Harpham, Geoffrey Galt. "Survival In and Of *The Painted Bird*: The Career of Jerzy Kosinski." *Georgia Review* 35.1 (1981): 142-57.

Describes the central problem of Kosinski's work as how to think about the unthinkable, the exoteric nature of his world, fictional technique as personal survival, the jungle metaphor at its base, and individual incidents demonstrating the survival of the boy. Ultimately connects the boy's experience to that of Western history. Discusses several other Kosinski works and concludes that it is we, despite our horror at him and his horror, that have conferred on Kosinski his fame and titles.

315. Heller, Terry. "Notes on Technique in Black Humor." *Thalia* 2.3 (1979): 15-21.

Provides an elaborate definition of the history and characteristics of black humor before proceeding to a discussion of its further refinements found in *The Painted Bird*.

316. Hidesaki, Yasuro. "Jerzy Kosinski's *The Painted Bird* as Holocaust Literature." *Kyushu American Literature* 26 (1985): 37-46.

Argues that few American writers, with the exception of Kosinski, have presented the full horrors of the holocaust. Suggests that Kosinski provides us with the outlines of the holocaust experience by describing primitivism, the atrocity and the remorselessness of extinction, even though he does not give us pictures of the gas chambers, forced labor camps, or crematoriums.

317. Hoffman, Gerhard. "Social Criticism and the Deformation of Man: Satire, the Grotesque and Comic Nihilism in the Modern and Postmodern American Novel." *Amerikastudien* 28.2 (1983): 141-203.

After a theoretical introduction into the aesthetics of satire, the grotesque and the comic, as well as into the aesthetic problems of meaning-building in the text, this essay sketches the history of fictional satire and the grotesque, including *The Painted Bird*.

318. Klinkowitz, Jerome, and David H. Richter. "Two Bibliographical Questions in Kosinski's *The Painted Bird*." *Contemporary Literature* 16.1 (1975): 126-29.

Points out some bibliographic errors in Richter's study "The Three Denouements of Jerzy Kosinski's *The Painted Bird*" [*Contemporary*

*Literature* 15.3 (1974): 370-85] created through differences in the various published versions of the novel in question provided by the author himself. Richter responds appreciatively to the "new light," but finds it doesn't appreciably alter his interpretation of the novel.

319. Lale, Meta, and John Williams. "The Narrator of *The Painted Bird*: A Case Study." *Renascence* 24.4 (1972): 198-206.

Claims *The Painted Bird* is primarily about a boy's odyssey through a world tainted with evil who finally becomes deranged. Shows how faced with this, the boy finally experiences withdrawal, fantasy, and introjection. Traces the psychopathology of the boy throughout the novel.

320. Landess, Thomas H. "The 'Snuff Film' and the Limits of Modern Aesthetics." *Literature and the Visual Arts in Contemporary Society.* Eds. Suzanne Ferguson and Barbara Groselclose. Columbus: Ohio State UP, 1985. 197-210.

Describes the genre of the sexually violent pornographic movie as eliminating the barrier between art and reality. Sees Kosinski as a literary artist who has managed the same end through the medium of language. Comments on the many critics who find his narratives akin to the pure and heightened sense of pain-in-sexuality that one finds only in the best of the sado-masochistic pornographers' art. A major article that develops this thesis in terms of *The Painted Bird*.

321. Langer, Lawrence L. "Men into Beasts." *The Holocaust and the Literary Imagination.* Lawrence L. Langer. New Haven: Yale UP, 1975. 167-91.

Discusses the conception of the holocaust and the technique of metaphor as an instrument of dehumanization in *The Painted Bird*. Sees its theme as humanity's inescapable complicity in evil so that in such a world man becomes a fugitive from all but his animal origins. Discusses the relationship of Dante's *Inferno* to this work and provides an excellent account of the major events of the novel. Chiefly concentrates on the transformation of men into beasts recounted throughout the work.

322. Loukides, Paul. "The Radical Vision." *Michigan Academician* 5.4 (1973): 497-503.

Argues that in *The Painted Bird* Kosinski traces out the rough history of Western mythology and demonstrates the inadequacy of each mythic system. Systematically covers each of the major events of the novel from this perspective. Concludes that for the reader willing to enter into a deviant world such as this without a baggage of fixed belief, these writers of the radical vision offer a sense of new worlds whose bounds are limited only by the human capacity to dream new dreams and embrace new mythologies.

323. McGinnis, Wayne D. "Transcendence and Primitive Sympathy in
     Kosinski's *The Painted Bird.*" *Studies in the Humanities* 8.1 (1980): 22-27.

     Takes Sir James Fraser's concept of sympathetic magic and Jungian con-
     cepts of regeneration to understand the kind of power and impulse at
     work in the Kosinski text. An interesting treatment of the protagonists of
     the novels.

324. Meszaros, Patricia K. "Hero with a Thousand Faces, Child with No Name:
     Kosinski's *The Painted Bird.*" *College Literature* 6 (1979): 232-44.

     Discusses the picaresque hero and his quest themes of freedom, survival,
     role playing, unusual birth, master-servant relationships, and his status as
     orphan as fundamental to a discussion of these elements in *The Painted
     Bird*. Claims that Kosinski recognized the coinherence of the picaresque
     mode and these archetypes as he planned the novel. Concludes that here
     the picaresque as a living mode has adapted itself to modern experience.

325. Mortimer, Gail L. "'Fear Death by Water': The Boundaries of the Self in
     Jerzy Kosinski's *The Painted Bird.*" *Psychoanalytic Review* 63.4 (1976):
     511-28.

     This paper, based on the psychoanalytic theory of R. D. Laing, shows the
     dilemma of the ontologically insecure person who becomes an inner self
     and a false outer self in response to specific dangers which threaten his
     existential experience.

326. Ozsvath, Zsuzsanna, and Martha Satz. "The Audacity of Expressing the
     Inexpressible: The Relation between Moral and Aesthetic Considerations
     in Holocaust Literature." *Judaism* 34.2 (1985): 197-210.

     Discusses the problems inherent in the subject of holocaust literature and
     provides an illustration of these problems in a discussion of *The Painted
     Bird*. Claims that the thesis of the treatment is Kosinski's statement, "My
     purpose in writing the novel was to examine a new language of brutality
     and its consequent new counter-language of anguish and despair."

327. Piwinski, David J. "Kosinski's *The Painted Bird.*" *Explicator* 40.1
     (1981): 62-63.

     Discusses Lekh's painting of the bird's wings and notes its futile
     attempts to rejoin the flock. Traces the source of this central metaphor to
     the Biblical verse from Jeremiah 12:9, "Mine heritage is unto me as a
     speckled bird, the birds round about her are against her; come ye, assem-
     ble all the beasts of the field, come to devour." Argues that since the
     passage is about the ravaging of Judah by the armies of the Moabites,
     Ammonites, and Edomites after 602 BC, clearly Kosinski is linking the
     boy's fate to that of his nation, Israel.

328.  Ricapito, Joseph V. "Jerzy Kosinski's *The Painted Bird* and the Picaresque Tradition." *Neohelicon* 5.2 (1977): 217-37.

Begins with Jose Ortega y Gasset's classic modern definition of the picaresque point-of-view as the rancorous view of the rogue looking up at a world to which he does not belong. Then applies this view to several of the novels. A major treatment of the subject. Concentrates mainly on *The Painted Bird*.

329.  Richter, David H. "The Reader as Ironic Victim." *Novel: A Forum on Fiction* 14.2 (1981): 135-51.

A major treatment of narrative irony which construes the reader as ironic victim. Briefly discusses *The Painted Bird* in this context and the effects of its sadism and violence on the reader.

330.  Richter, David H. "The Three Denouements of Jerzy Kosinski's *The Painted Bird*." *Contemporary Literature* 15.3 (1974): 370-85.

Describes the textual variations in the three editions of *The Painted Bird* and the three different readings based on the revised endings or denouements.

331.  Rider, Philip R. "The Three States of the Text of Kosinski's *The Painted Bird*." *Papers of the Bibliographical Society of America* 72.3 (1978): 361-84.

An erudite account of Kosinski's comments on the inception of the novel, its critical reception, and its printing history. Mostly concentrates on the textual differences and meanings between the three variant editions.

332.  Sewell, Ernestine P. "The Jungian Process of Individuation as Structure in *The Painted Bird*." *South Central Bulletin* 38.4 (1978): 160-63.

Applies the constructs of the Jungian individuation process to *The Painted Bird* by outlining the entire mythic pattern of the novel. Concludes that to recognize the Jungian apparatus for interpretation of the "mirror of humanity" that folk culture affords is to recognize the classic worth of *The Painted Bird*.

333.  Skau, Michael, Michael Carroll, and Donald Cassiday. "Jerzy Kosinski's *The Painted Bird*: A Modern Bestiary." *Polish Review* 27.3-4 (1982): 45-54.

Describes the thematic and functional use of animals in the text to establish the tenor of the novel and to stipulate a world of violence and terror. Concludes: "Kosinski's novel reveals human behavior to be at least as bestial as what we would expect from "mere" animals."

334.  Spendal, R. J. "The Structure of *The Painted Bird*." *Journal of Narrative Technique* 6.1 (1976): 132-36.

Describes twenty chapters of the novel as organized into two groups of ten with corresponding chapters in each group linked by the principle of parallel-with-contrast. Also demonstrates this and deals with the thematic implications of these binary patterns.

335. Weales, Gerald. "Jerzy Kosinski: *The Painted Bird* and Other Disguises." *Hollins Critic* 9.3 (1972): 1-12.

A generalized and useful introduction to Kosinski, his world, the reactions of the critics, the books, his style, and his thematic concerns. An excellent overview.

336. Ziegler, Robert E. "The Disconnected Eye: Vision and Retribution in Kosinski's *The Painted Bird*." *Par Rapport* 5-6 (1982-83): 67-70.

Provides a detailed account of the contents of the novel without developing a particular thesis.

# Reviews

337. Allen, Trevor. "On Expatriates." *Books and Bookmen* Apr. 1966: 40.

Describes the horrifying incidents of the story and questions whether it is a true story rather than the "fevered creation of an imagination, partly founded on experience." Finds the writing powerful and the contents stark.

338. Arimond, John. "Engrossing Sociological Novel." *Extension* [Chicago] Mar. 1966: 47.

Recounts the biographical contents of The Painted Bird and notes that the vivid picture of the curious brand of religion in this Eastern European tradition will be of most interest to sophisticated American Catholic readers. Describes the intermingling of Roman Catholicism and deep-seated pagan superstition. Concludes that this is an engrossing historical and sociological portrait.

339. Ascherson, Neal. "Chronicles of the Holocaust." *New York Review of Books* 1 June 1967: 25.

Considers this novel a fable about the presence of Hell in Heaven and the proximity of filth and savagery to innocence and delight. Discusses Holocaust accounts in general and declares this a truthful one.

340. Bauke, Joseph P. "No Wakening from Nightmare." *Saturday Review* 13 Nov. 1965: 64.

Calls this novel a book of terrifying impact replete with scenes of sadism rarely matched in contemporary writing. Claims that Kosinski evokes with the grim precision of a dream a world of Gothic monstrosities.

Concludes that there is sincerity in the book but that it is not of the imagination's making. Sees Kosinski as the master of the macabre and an authentic voice of the century.

341. Coles, Robert. "Book Reviews." *Harvard Educational Review* 37.3 (1967): 493-96. Rpt. as "The Song of the Painted Bird" in *That Red Wheelbarrow: Selected Literary Essays*. Robert Coles. Iowa City: U of Iowa P, 1988. 87-92.

Describes this century and its history of brutality to children. Commends *The Painted Bird* for its unusual form and content. Describes the contents in detail, noting its brilliant and unnerving characteristics that invite us to speculate on the theological, moral, educational, and psychological implications of such stories. Sees this boy's story as the untold story of millions of children.

342. Compton, Neil. "Dream of Violence." *Commentary* June 1966: 92-5.

Sees *The Painted Bird* as belonging to the last wave of war novels like Gunter Grass' *Tin Drum* which provide autobiographical accounts of the suffering of children during the war. Notes that the juxtaposition of childish innocence and the most brutal forms of fallen adult experience produce a myth of uncommon intensity. Provides an account of the story and its backdrop—Poland.

343. Davenport, Guy. "Messages from the Lost." *National Review* 8 Feb. 1966: 120-21.

Calls *The Painted Bird* a book about the violence and ignorance of war without any prurience or gratuitousness. Suggests that it is a heartbreaking novel that seems to argue that man is the only perverted animal and the only one capable of perverting himself. Concludes that this book should only be recommended to the strong of stomach, but that at least they ought to read it.

344. Evanier, David. *Commonweal* 1 July 1966: 422-23.

Begins with the observation that concentration camp literature has penetrated the consciousness of all and that this novel of Kosinski's, which takes place outside the concentration camp, nevertheless makes the connections between the evils of the outer world and those of the inner, private world. Labels it a deeply moral work.

345. Field, Andrew. "The Butcher's Helpers." *New York Herald Tribune Book Week* 17 Oct. 1965: 2-3, 26.

Describes the contents of the novel as atrocities that are almost unreadable, projects the Polish reaction to the book, describes the symbolic import of the painted bird, and lists the atrocities committed by the boys after the war. Commends its high literary merit, and details Kosinski's reaction to postwar communism.

346. Halley, Anne. "Poor Boy Spreads His Wings." *Nation* 29 Nov. 1965: 424-26.

Calls the novel a survivor tale crossed with the lost child genre of children's fairy tales. Develops a picture of the literary antecedents of the story, recounts the plot, and lists all the archetypal fairy tale elements.

347. Kamm, Henry. "Poles are Bitter about Novel Published Abroad." *New York Times* 12 Dec. 1966: 2.

Describes the Polish response to the novel despite the fact that no copy was available. Lists the responses of many newspapers and journals. A brief but important record of this response.

348. Kluger, Richard. "A Scapegoat in Need." *Harper's* Oct. 1965: 128-30.

Describes the plot and details several instances of the cruelty the boy protagonist suffered and observed among the peasants of Eastern Poland. Considers it "an utterly dispassionate recounting of desperate acts, unadorned by moral reflection or self-pitying lamentation."

349. Pine, John C. "Reviews." *199 Ways to Review a Book*. John C. Pine. Metuchen: Scarecrow, 1971. 239-40. Rpt. from *Smithtown Messenger*.

A brief account of the contents, setting, and style of the novel. Concludes that what the book really conveys is not a literal account of a small boy's experiences, but a heightened account of his impressions of man's inhumanity to man.

350. Poore, Charles. "Things Like These Happen to People We Know." *New York Times* 16 Oct. 1965: 25.

Calls the nightmare world of *The Painted Bird* a timeless corner of Goya's "Disasters of War." Sees Kosinski shredding our composure with accounts of the grotesqueness and shabbiness of lust. Details the contents.

351. Ryan, F. L. "Fiction." *Best Sellers* 1 Nov. 1965: 299.

Describes the contents of the novel as brutal. Sees his art as referential and accomplished through brutal symbolic structures and reflections integrated with events. Complains that other writers have observed and recorded the horrors of war and life without the gratuitous details.

352. Wiesel, Elie. "Everybody's Victim." *New York Times Book Review* 31 Oct. 1965: 5, 46.

Considers Kosinski a writer who asks not to be understood, but merely to be heard and believed. Calls this novel a book of unusual power. Details the contents.

353. Zeldis, Chayym. "Job, the Child." *Jewish Frontier* Mar. 1967: 22-26.

A laudatory review that claims everyone should read this book in order to be called civilized. Primarily recounts the contents of the book.

# Passion Play

354. Nass, Barry. "Androgyny, Transsexuality, and Transgression in Jerzy Kosinski's *Passion Play.*" *Contemporary Literature* 31.1 (1990): 37-57.

Argues that the shocking transsexuality and androgyny in *Passion Play* between Fabian, Manuela, and others is not merely sensational. Sees it as an incisive exploration of gender identity, sexual change, and androgyny in conflict with the values of a patriarchal culture. Claims the relationship epitomizes Kosinski's enduring concern with the struggle for self-understanding and the affirmation of selfhood in a world hostile to the individual and the expression of personal freedom.

355. Shinitzky, Ami. "Life Is a Drama—Jerzy Kosinski: The Man and His Work." *Polo* Dec. 1979: 21-23, 44.

Provides details about Kosinski's life and career, but concentrates primarily on his use of polo playing in *Passion Play*. Recounts the plot interspersed with quotations from the novel. Concludes that polo players reading this novel have an advantage over other readers because they not only learn what polo means to Kosinski and Fabian, but gain also a knowledge of the fictional people, places, and events inspired by the real.

## Reviews

356. Ableman, Paul. "The Champ." *Spectator* 19 Apr. 1980: 19-20.

Describes how Fabian in *Passion Play* is a combination of American cowboy and hustler as well as European hero as knight. Develops this thesis along with the assessment that it is an irritating, powerful, silly, inconsistent, heterogeneous work whose slightly decadent depths just hint at genius.

357. Cheuse, Alan. "Books in Brief." *Saturday Review* 19 Jan. 1980: 52-53.

Argues that in *Passion Play*, Kosinski's eleventh novel, there is the usual protagonist whose life is a series of disconnected steps leading nowhere, women who are more vagina than mind, existential meditations, and explicitly described physical torture.

358. Cunningham, Valentine. "Let it Bleed." *Times Literary Supplement* 25 Apr. 1980: 470.

Provides a detailed treatment of the character of Fabian in *Passion Play*. Comments on the stylistic effects of the novel, its violence, its explicitness, sexual violence, and "flighted bursts of rhetoric."

359. Gilder, Joshua. "Existential Cowboy Gone Astray." *New Leader* 19 Nov. 1979: 19-20.

Describes the hero of *Passion Play* as mellow compared with earlier protagonists, yet full of consuming aggression turned inward, modulated into neurotic self-absorption with the body and sickness. Complains of the boring sexual descriptions, likening them to *Penthouse* and finds his forays into lyrical description embarrassing. Concludes that this is really only the stuff of adolescent romance.

360. Gold, Ivan. "Picaresque Sport." *New York Times Book Review* 30 Sept. 1979: 9, 18.

Describes the novel as picaresque and its protagonist as a knight-errant. Provides a detailed account of the contents of the book.

361. Kanfer, Stefan. "When Going Is the Goal." *Time* 17 Sept. 1979: 105.

Calls *Passion Play* a picaresque in which adolescents, sophisticates, and transsexuals are all given equal time. Describes the prose as purely disfigured centerfold and indistinguishable from Harold Robbins' paragraphs. Complains that Kosinski writes powerful interludes only to vandalize them by reducing his characters to prototypes. Comments on his unparalleled ear for language and eye for social nuance, and wonders if they will be used solely for the exploration of the same theme of aimlessness.

362. Kennedy, William. "Kosinski's Hero Rides On." *Washington Post Book World* 16 Sept. 1979: 1, 11.

Describes *Passion Play* as a book without nostalgia but with an earned poignancy, a continuation of the struggles of the boy from *The Painted Bird* losing his hair and entering into a crisis of middle-age and lost youth. Claims he is wilfully lyrical in places and works with a more than usually developed plot. Provides a detailed discussion on the evolution of the Kosinski hero.

363. Koning, Hans. "Missions Impossible." *Nation* 15 Sept. 1979: 216-18.

Reviews Kosinski's life, his early novels, typical themes, and political views. Describes *Passion Play* as a book that hammers home all the earlier material, depicting as it does so the loveless, joyless world of Eastern Europe. Criticizes him for the unfriendly light he throws on Eastern Europe and for misuse of the Charles Manson killings. Notes that he ultimately superimposes a mechanized view of a crime-racked individualism onto an Eastern European model whose commonality does nothing but lay it open to a cannibalistic sense of power. Concludes that in such a world we are indeed left with little to hope for except to be left alone. The Grail knight of earlier novels is here pursuing "polo."

364. LaHood, Marvin J. "Fiction." *World Literature Today* 54.2 (1980): 282.

Finds that at times Kosinski's writing skill fuses with his perceptions, but notes this novel lacking in any loftiness or profundity. Sees the style as staccato and unrelenting and finally embodies a gray view of the joyless, loveless, human condition. Concludes that a novel that sees only the false and hollow din of life becomes superficial and uninteresting.

365. Lawson, Carol. "Behind the Best Sellers." *New York Times Book Review* 21 Oct. 1979: 58.

Contains a mixture of familiar anecdotes and a few remarks about *Passion Play,* along with some information about Kosinski's lifestyle and methods of writing.

366. Lupack, Barbara Tepa. "Book Reviews." *Polish Review* 25.3-4 (1980): 116-17.

Describes the character of Fabian as an older version of the mute boy of *The Painted Bird.* Considers parts of the novel stirring and romantic, while others contain familiar scenes of sex and violence, violent sex, and the need to control. Concludes that like such themes and treatments or not, Kosinski is a major force in the modern novel.

367. Mano, D. Keith. "Big Reject." *National Review* 12 Oct. 1979: 1312-13.

Complains that if this is the book that has just won the National Book Award, "he hasn't felt so chapfallen since he found out that Salisbury steak was no more than a social climbing quarter-pounder." Complains sarcastically and bitterly that *Passion Play* is shabby, written with painstaking negligence, and proof of Kosinski's God-given flair for mediocrity.

368. Prescott, Peter S. "A Horse Story for Grown-ups." *Newsweek* 10 Sept. 1979: 73.

Describes *Passion Play* as an adolescent erotic fantasy, part myth, part psychological dominion. Complains that Kosinski has not yet resolved problems of tone and credibility. Notes that despite the fact that this is possibly portentous stuff, it really belongs to the squalid club. Concludes that Kosinski takes great risks with unconventional modes of narrative and characterization.

369. Reist, John S., Jr. "A Mere 'Picaro'." *Christian Century* 30 Jan. 1980: 112-14.

Admires *Passion Play* for its erotic descriptions, powerfully evoked polo matches, and plotting strategy. Criticizes his missing the mark with a title metaphor that fails, sexist attitudes, failure to create Fabian beyond a picaro, failure to produce adequate secondary characters, and one-sided women.

370. Yourgrau, Barry. "Short Circuits." *Village Voice* 24 Sept. 1979: 48.

Calls *Passion Play* a stiff-necked new novel about sports, sex, and the will to freedom and self-knowledge, and an intensely alone man. Describes the contents of the novel and notes that it is written in a conspicuous and relentlessly "fine" style that ultimately impedes the narrative as it becomes a series of dense, set pieces, sloppy and baroque.

# Pinball

371. Gorskowska, Regina. "Pinball: Aspects of Visibility: An Interview with Jerzy Kosinski." *Society for the Fine Arts Review* 4.2 (1982): 3-4.

    In this interview Kosinski explains *Pinball*, his latest novel, as standing outside the circle of the other novels. He discusses the hostile reviews the novel has generated, describes the reviewing process, talks about the central character of the novel and its central metaphor—invisibility. He also discusses the Jack Henry Abbott incident, his early reading of Tillich and Heschel, and his subsequent decision to be a writer.

## Reviews

372. Bangs, Lester. "Brief Encounters." *Village Voice* 16 Mar. 1982: 43.

    Calls *Pinball* an unreadable novel with a ludicrous plot, unbelievable cartoon characters, leaden dialogue, melodramatic tone, and prolix sex scenes. Details contents.

373. Bigsby, Christopher. "Coercive Plots." *Times Educational Supplement* 6 Aug. 1982: 17.

    Considers that Kosinski follows Zola's dictum that a writer should be as cold as a vivisectionist at a lecture. Calls his themes obsessive, plots elaborate, and characters isolated. Sees *Pinball* as an extension of that process in which there is an impulse to create coercive plots that threaten the integrity of self, but which also celebrate the resistant imagination.

374. DeMott, Benjamin. "Grand Guignol with Music." *New York Times Book Review* 7 Mar. 1982: 8.

    Recounts the contents of *Pinball*, and calls it a descent into self-indulgent laxness. It is depressingly flat, ridden with pulpish Grand Guignol," exceptionally high in cliche density, and packed with screaming sex partners. Concludes that most visible on any page is the spectacle of self-imprisonment—a writer locked into a cage through which no glimpse of the living common world can be caught. Finally sees it as a sadly unrewarding book.

375. Emerson, Sally. "Recent Fiction." *Illustrated London News* July 1982: 61.

    Claims that *Pinball* is about alienation, random violence, and perverse sex. Notes that although the novel is entertaining in the most undemanding way, there is a sense of emptiness as the rusty machinery of plot and character creaks away along the familiar path.

376. Fetherling, Doug. "Sex and Dreams and Rock'n'Roll." *MacLean's* 8 Mar. 1982: 64-65.

Sees *Pinball* as a book whose social commentary on urban anthropology is unfortunately undermined by a disintegrating plot in what amounts to an ersatz mystery. Notes that the narrative flow is maintained only for the first half of the book, then the whole thing dissolves into silly coincidences. Concludes that in the end, the subject of the book overwhelms the style.

377. Gilder, Joshua. "Fiction Briefs." *Saturday Review* Mar. 1982: 63-64.

Calls Kosinski an important author, and reasons that he must have written an important book in writing *Pinball*. Suggests, however, that if its meager plot strikes the reader as serious, such a reader deserves to read the book because it is nothing more than a pornographic thriller.

378. Kanfer, Stefan. "Trebles." *Time* 22 Mar. 1982: 84, 87.

Discusses Kosinski's habitual use of metaphor in previous novels and now in *Pinball*. Details the contents of the story, comments that he provides saline comments about American life, deftly lampoons contemporary lyrics, and provides scenes from South Bronx life that seem torn from a Bosch triptych. Concludes: "What a premise?" "What talent!" "What a waste!"

379. Mars-Jones, Adam. "Rolling over Chopin." *Times Literary Supplement* 28 May 1982: 579.

Describes *Pinball* as a thriller somewhat spoiled by the author's habits of scattering opinions and values all over the book. Condemns the work as flashy and mechanical.

380. McLellan, Joseph. "Playing at Life." *Washington Post Book World* 7 Mar. 1982: 7.

Claims that *Pinball* displays uncommon familiarity with music and the music business and that he clearly uses his friends as well as his mother's career as a concert pianist. Complains that the characters are treated as objects and that intense feeling is on a microscopic scale. Notes also that beneath all of this the feelings seem too hot to be approached closely. Concludes that the all-persuasive relationship displayed is that of victim and victimizer.

381. Rogers, Pat. "Ambassadors." *London Review of Books* 3-16 June 1982: 18-19.

Sees *Pinball* as totally unsubtle, pointless, and full of irrelevant paragraphs. Details the contents and pans Kosinski's style.

# Steps

382. Boyers, Robert. "Language and Reality in Kosinski's *Steps.*" *Centennial Review* 16.1 (1972): 41-61. Rpt. in *Excursions: Selected Literary Essays.* Robert Boyers. Literary Criticism Series. Port Washington: Kennikat, 1977. 71-86.

A discussion of *Steps* which argues that the book's structure eludes the usual forms of structural analysis criticism performs since it is neither symbolic nor realistic. Claims it should be judged by the weight it applies to our sensibilities and denies it is either humanistic or philosophical. Concludes with a major treatment of themes, techniques, and effects in the book.

383. Bruss, Paul. "Steps: Acts of Demystification." *Victims: Textual Strategies in Recent American Fiction.* Paul Bruss. Lewisburg: Bucknell U P, 1981. 183-97.

Argues that Kosinski's readers are ultimately forced to interpret his fiction in terms of their own language because inevitably they become aware of the terms of a new discourse which challenges the nature of the values they bring to the reading. Thus he demystifies the grammar and syntax of everyday language to force the reader to an awareness of its limits. Provides a lengthy and erudite discussion of *Steps.* Concludes that the best the narrator or reader can hope for is a "shrewd awareness of the intricate processes of language in his own life."

384. Daler, John Kent von. "An Introduction to Jerzy Kosinski's *Steps.*" *Language and Literature* 1.1 (1971): 43-49.

Describes the book as divided between a series of steps and flights, connected by the "I" sensibility, whose only stable characteristic seems to be his masculinity. Suggests that *Steps* is an exercise in control with its tight, sparse, striking style. Concludes that it is the reader who imposes form, and hails Kosinski as a latter-day Sterne.

385. Gardner, John. "The Way We Write Now." *New York Times Book Review* 9 July 1972: 2, 32.

A speculative essay on the nature of American fiction with some references to Nabokov and Kosinski. Argues that although Kosinski believes his business is language and that he is the sole creator of his fictive world, the typically American theme of the idea of the damned and the saved is American as it reveals itself in *Steps.*

386. Harper, Howard M., Jr. "Trends in Recent American Fiction." *Contemporary Literature* 12.2 (1971): 213-14.

A discussion of *Steps* which illuminates its psychodynamics of violence and sadism. Discusses also the twin streams of narrative, the theme of control, the odyssey from the old world to the new, its Grand Guignol horror, and the limited human range of episodes which don't permit the whole truth to emerge.

387. Hutchinson, James D. "Retrospect: Judging a Book Award." *Denver Quarterly* 4.3 (1969): 128-35.

Notes that *Steps* is deserving of its National Book Award and comments on its subtle, poetic style, effective structure, and depth of character analysis. Describes the inward odyssey of the book, its universality, use of time, protagonist, key incidents, emotions, and techniques.

388. Klinkowitz, Jerome. "Literary Disruptions; or, What's Become of American Fiction?" *Partisan Review* 40.3 (1973): 433-44.

Argues that in *Steps* Kosinski gives 150 pages and over forty episodes in apparently random juxtaposition, a search back through blackened memories for the original innocent self. Claims the strategy is an immersion in the heart of the trauma itself. Describes several of the novels in this way.

389. Petrakis, Byron. "Jerzy Kosinski's *Steps* and the Cinematic Novel." *Comparatist* 2 (1978): 16-22.

Describes Kosinski's skills as a photographer and his association with filmmaker Roman Polanski. Details such effects as panning, montage, sequences of edited images, the cinematic image, use of master symbols, connotative and denotative language, the depersonalization of modern cinematic images, and the visual effects of his novels. Links him with contemporary European-style movie-making technique and image making.

390. Rosenberg, Marc. "*Steps.*" Audio Cassette. Deland: Everett/Edwards, 1971.

391. Walker, Kenneth E. "*Steps.*" *Survey of Contemporary Literature*. Ed. Frank N. Magill. Rev. ed. 12 vols. Englewood Cliffs: Salem, 1977. 11: 7224-26.

A standard reference article on *Steps* covering the principal characters, Kosinski's publishing history, the contents, and its style.

# Reviews

392. "Album from Auschwitz." *Times Literary Supplement* 8 May 1969: 481.

Comments that *Steps* is full of desperate knowledge and cold fantasy of violent extremes. Suggests that this is dangerous, if true, and pretentious, if not. Doubts the arrangement of the material and its ultimate value.

393. Bailey, Paul. "'Stuff' and Nonsense." *London Magazine* May 1969: 108, 110, 112.

     Calls *Steps* a terrifying saga of man's attempt to define himself through acts of pure violence and extreme sexuality. Provides a sarcastic series of comments on the sexual antics in the novel, and denounces the whole thing as a pretty ordinary piece of sub-Kafka. Considers it formless, witless, self-admiring, without craft, and generally incoherent.

394. Baker, Roger. "Off-Beat Ideas." *Books and Bookmen* July 1969: 41-42.

     Comments on the novel's cinematic elements and internal structure. Praises the language and outlines the contents.

395. "Bird of Prey." *Time* 18 Oct. 1968: 114.

     Calls *Steps* an account of the consequences of a childhood schooled by atrocities. Notes the disconnected episodes and the Gogol-like treatment of communism. Suggests that the purity of the book is savage, and the effects hypnotic but short lived. Concludes that it lacks the grounding, structure, and persuasion that could have made it more than a rather abstract expression of a pathological mind.

396. Blumenfeld, F. Yorick. "Dark Dreams." *Newsweek* 21 Oct. 1968: 104, 108.

     Calls *Steps* indigenous, expatriate Polish literature hovering on the margins of reality and dealing in intellectual, artistic, and moral paradox. Claims this book is held together by a compelling lack of conscience. Suggests that this is more than a novel; this is a collection of erotic reminiscences, a log of the outrageous that seems at first to be reality itself. Concludes that finally, the reader is overwhelmed by all sorts of wishful erotic fantasies.

397. Capitanchik, Maurice. "Private Lives." *Spectator* 9 May 1969: 621.

     Complains that *Steps* contains grotesque and brutal sexual experiences all interspersed with coldly sensual dialogue. Concludes that this is the dream of the sensationalist, that most fruitless of all idealists, the man without moral imagination. Condemns Kosinski's attempt to strip the human face of its mask of hypocrisy while being devoid of knowledge of love's concerns and of humor.

398. Felheim, Marvin. "The Haunted Edges of Consciousness." *Michigan Daily* 24 Nov. 1968: 6.

     Finds Kosinski a product of two significant literary traditions: he is an Eastern European writing in English and a writer of stories of horror and the grotesque. In these traditions he follows in the footsteps of Conrad, Nabokov, Hawthorne, Poe, Dickens, Kafka, and Dinesen. Discusses the quality of his prose and his use of language. Concludes that Kosinski uses bestiality, sado-masochism, and other monstrosities to create not only a genuine sense of horror, but an "implied plea for consideration and sympathy."

399. Fremont-Smith, Eliot. "Log of Atrocities." *New York Times* 21 Oct. 1968: 45.

Calls *Steps* a book constructed of about three-dozen brief episodes in which the narrator witnesses or participates in a variety of brutalities—sexual, political, emotional, and physical. Notes the narrator's disinterested bystander role and the hard, gemlike, lucid prose. Concludes that this is a profoundly disturbing book, gratuitous in its brutality, but engaged in charting a territory where nothing except human possibility encompasses hell—the proof of this being our ability to imagine it.

400. Furbank, P. N. "Fiction's Feelingless Man." *Listener* 8 May 1969: 655.

Claims *Steps* is written in the tradition of Dostoevsky, Sade, Camus, Mailer, and the theater of cruelty. Yet suggests there is nothing gothic or gloating in the telling of the episodes, no matter how bestial they are because they drop into the mind with the indifference they impact on the hero. Concludes that Kosinski is a novelist to take seriously.

401. Hicks, Granville. "Sadism and Light Hearts." *Saturday Review* 19 Oct. 1968: 29.

Describes the impact he felt when reading Kosinski's first novel *The Painted Bird* and finds the narrator of *Steps* to be the boy grown up and the story to demonstrate the deformation of character created by the "outrageous cruelty" depicted in the earlier work. Describes some of the sadistic sexual episodes, and concludes that the world depicted here "is one in which anything is permitted and nothing is much fun."

402. Howe, Irving. "From the Other Side of the Moon." *Harpers* Mar. 1969: 102-05.

Discusses the prose of *Steps* as pungent and disciplined and the book as experimental and highly problematic in aesthetic strategy. Outlines the characters and contents of the novel, the setting, and the series of bizarre episodes which are designed not simply to shock but to strip bare the inattention of the reader. Finds these the standard repertoire of the modern. Describes the structure, pattern of images, and the brilliant language of the book. Concludes that the evil Kosinski records is not of his making.

403. Jackson, Katherine Gauss. "Books in Brief." *Harper's* Nov. 1968: 160.

Calls *Steps* an offensive piece whose author tells of shocking, violent, sexual experiences with unemotional vividness. Suggests that the power comes from the author always present as voyeur or participant. Concludes that what the steps mean or where they lead is not discernable.

404. Jones, D. A. N. "Lean Creatures." *New York Review of Books* 27 Feb. 1969: 16-18.

Calls *Steps* a painful collection of Goya-like etchings done in chill prose recalling Thom Gunn's verse that also reflects the imagination of a post-war adolescence. Suggests that Kosinski's surreal landscape combines aspects of Central Europe and the U.S., i.e., impersonal countryside and ungoverned cities where strangers may gang up on you.

405. Jones, Richard. "Patterns of Obsession." *Times* 10 May 1969: 21.

Finds in this novel the same bestiality, viciousness, and revenge as in *The Painted Bird*. Briefly describes the story. Concludes that if readers find the themes revolting, they must enjoy the "pellucid, subtle style" or stop reading it, for the final effect is "convoluted negativity."

406. Jordan, Clive. "Big 70." *New Statesman* 9 May 1969: 665-66.

Complains of no underlying progression in the episodes in *Steps*, which he says is a violent, literary *Mondo Cane*. Describes the style as abstract realism, icily scientific curiosity, all assuming a random malignity in the world.

407. Kauffmann, Stanley. "Out of the Fires." *New Republic* 26 Oct. 1968: 22, 41.

Argues that in *Steps*, Kosinski breaks with the traditional novel by making the book scorchingly personal. Describes the book's fifty episodes arranged in eight numbered sections, some linked in content, some unified in vision. Describes the settings as metaphorical and the chronology as disturbed. Discusses Jewishness and questions male phallic power. Concludes that it is a novel about terror, killing, political travesties, and the scraping out of small plateaus of tranquility.

408. Kenner, Hugh. "Keys on a Ring." *New York Times Book Review* 20 Oct. 1968: 5.

Describes *Steps* as a low-keyed, efficient, controlled piece of prose encompassing the banal, the picturesque, and the monstrous with never a flicker of surprise. Concludes that this is a book composed of memories about cruelty, ritual, and restless love.

409. McAleer, John J. "Fiction." *Best Sellers* 15 Oct. 1968: 316.

Describes this novel as a series of self-contained episodes connected by the theme of sex, revenge, capricious murder, or twisted charity. Claims the book exhibits "every picturable aberration in human sexual behavior and Kosinski's view that "life is a pursuit of awareness." Finds *Steps* like walking on a treadmill, "a very existential way to travel," as the protagonist steps on people in his unsuccessful efforts for requital.

410. Mudrick, Marvin. "Must We Burn Mme. de Beauvoir?" *Hudson Review* 21.4 (1968-69): 759-60.

While reviewing a variety of novels, Mudrick discusses *Steps* and its famous gang-rape scene, recounts the horrors of Kosinski's childhood, and condemns *The Painted Bird* for ending in a blare of crude socialist realism. Concludes that reading Kosinski is like reading 3,000 pages of Marquis de Sade—a major illness ensues.

411. O'Malley, Michael. *Critic* Apr.-May 1969: 76.

Complains that this book exults in the cruel power of man over his flesh and his sex. Argues that it derides innocence and sanctifies despair, while locating essential truth in man's life, wants, and compulsions. Notes that it is well-written, comprised of a series of episodes, and narrated by a priest of cruelty. Concludes that "while ideas—good or bad—come from whole men. Only saints of depravity—not the voyeurs, not the dirty little boys—can tell us how it is. This book doesn't."

412. Stark, Irwin. "The Agonies of Survival." *Hadassah Magazine* Mar 1969: 19.

Calls Steps less a novel than a document because the writer expects us to provide the emotion appropriate for such a catalogue of horrors. Concludes that the novel fails as fiction.

413. Stern, Daniel. "An Old Evil Moves Westward." *Life* 6 Dec. 1968: 24.

Describes *Steps* as an account from the non-parochial regions of zeroland—the Holocaust. Sees this book as a melange of adventures in nameless lands narrated by a nameless man who meets nameless orphans. Suggest that this is the world of total alienation, of impulse freed from convention—in short the cruel kind of world that is a legacy of the 20th century.

414. Tucker, Martin. "A Moralist's Journey into the Heart of Darkness." *Commonweal* 29 Nov. 1968: 319-20.

Calls *Steps* a *tour de force* with a nameless "I" through whom Kosinski explores the idea of identity and how certain people manage to deny another's identity. Also sees it as a novel about control in which the hero tries to gauge how much cruelty, love, and sadism he is able to will into his experiences. Describes the contents.

415.  West, Paul. "Portrait of a Man Mooning." *Chicago Tribune Book World*
      3 Nov. 1968: 18.

      Describes *Steps* as a ladder set up as a see-saw upon which a lascivious-
      minded matter-of-fact descendant of Coleridge's Ancient Mariner totters
      between two extremes: the unmentioned years preceding the hero's stu-
      dent days and what reads like his eventual departure beyond the Iron
      Curtain. Comments on the uneveness of the novel and Kosinski's pecu-
      liar style.

416.  Wolff, Geoffrey. "Growing Poisonous Flowers." *New Leader* 7 Oct.
      1968: 18-19.

      Wolff notes *Steps*'s morbid, cruel, perverse, and salacious contents and
      asks, "To what is art morally responsible?" Lists the contents of the
      book: bestiality, lustless seduction, male prostitution, female prostitution,
      homosexual prostitution, many kinds of rape, pandery, revenge, incest,
      and criminality. Feels the novel goes far beyond guilt, while totally
      ignoring love. Complains that ultimately the book has no symbolic life
      and no resonance. Concludes that a fragile barrier separates psychosis
      from aesthetics, and that Kosinski has abandoned art and abused artistic
      power.

417.  Young, Tracy. "On Jerzy Kosinski." *Mademoiselle* Aug. 1973: 68, 77.

      Calls *Steps* a repugnant book, morbid, cruel, and perverse, even sala-
      cious. Yet also commends it for being precise, scrupulous, poetic, and
      shockingly cool. Suggests that ultimately it is a beautifully written book.
      Concludes with a statement about the fragile balance that divides psy-
      chosis and aesthetics.

# Reviews of Nonfiction Books

418. Chamberlin, William Henry. "Firsthand Impressions of How the Soviet Mind Works." Rev. of *No Third Path*. *Chicago Sunday Tribune* 25 Feb. 1962: 4.

Briefly describes several conversations from the book, notes the general theme of subservience to the collective in all aspects of Soviet life, and concludes that this is one of the best collections of "raw material" on life and the mind in Russia, but would have been improved with more analysis by the author.

419. Crankshaw, Edward. "Reporting on Russia." Rev. of *The Future Is Ours, Comrade: Conversations with the Russians*. *Observer* 30 Oct. 1960: 22.

Describes the author as a citizen of a Russian satellite country who knows little about Russian history or government policy—an advantage in reporting his interviews. Suggests that his humor is deficient, his knowledge of human nature blindly ignorant, and that he has no eye for people. Claims the book gives us the underside of the carpet where the pattern doesn't show. Feels many respondents were adopting a cloak of orthodoxy and misleading the young interviewer, but that the book gives clearly the mechanics of Soviet society and is "a genuine contribution."

420. Harrison, Joseph G. "'Conversations with the Russians'." Rev. of *The Future Is Ours, Comrade: Conversations with the Russians*. *Christian Science Monitor* 25 May 1960: 13.

Finds this a "grim and fascinating book." Describes the kinds of people Kosinski conversed with and the picture of Russian life that emerges, which includes weaknesses in the Soviet system as well as Russians' insistence that the communist system will win against capitalism both economically and militarily. Suggests this book be read thoughtfully and carefully.

421. Hottelet, Richard C. "From Collective to Kremlin, It's One Big State of Nerves." Rev. of *The Future Is Ours, Comrade: Conversations with the Russians*. *New York Times Book Review* 22 May 1960: 3.

Here Russians reveal details of their lives and thoughts in conversations with Kosinski. Shows how the picture of Soviet life that emerges, even in this post-Stalinist era, is one of bureaucratic control, conformity, and obedience. People are submerged in the collective where they are watched, reported on by the house committee, the factory, union, school, army and party, and their lives are determined by the state. Finds the book an interesting personal document, important for the first-hand testimonies that allow readers to draw their own conclusions. Hottelet sees only a "drab, dank nightmare" as the future for Russians.

422. Jaskievicz, Walter C. "Non-Fiction." Rev. of *The Future Is Ours, Comrade: Conversations with the Russians*. *Best Sellers* 15 June 1960: 113.

This book attempts to answer the question of what Russians are thinking and whether they are for or against communism by reporting Kosinski's conversations with Russians. Describes some of the views the Russians have about housing, conformity, the pervasive guilt complex, and the change of humans to animals.

423. Jorden, William J. "Collective Ways of Being." Rev. of *The Future Is Ours, Comrade: Conversations with the Russians*. *New Leader* 24 Oct. 1960: 24-25.

Describes the way in which Kosinski did his research in Russia through interviewing Russians and recording their views. Describes how he reports on their attitudes and feelings about the government, their feeling that war with capitalism is inevitable, and that the Soviet Union would win, the web of control that surrounds everyone, and anti-Semitism. Concludes that this work is not intended to be definitive but that it abounds in information not available to most outsiders.

424. O'Connor, William. "Non-Fiction." Rev. of *No Third Path*. *Best Sellers* 1 Mar. 1962: 479-80.

Sees this as another work similar to *The Future Is Ours, Comrade* based on conversations with middle-class Russians. Shows how these conversations contrast the Stalinist government terror with the post-Stalinist terror exercised by the collective, the trade union, neighbors, or the youth society. Describes both as attempts to keep citizens under control, and the best defense is to get lost in the middle of the crowd where you won't be noticed. Discusses the unreality of "socialist realism," and notes the fact that these conversants talk about "a whole clutch of ideas." Notes that scholars may prefer to read other works on the Soviet society and mentality, but that this book is "full of the thrills of discovery."

425. Pisko, Ernest S. "A Condition of Super-Integration." Rev. of *No Third Path*. *Christian Science Monitor* 13 Apr. 1962: 15.

Describes Kosinski's background and his growing awareness that while living in Eastern Europe that communism was destructive of human character. Describes the author's examples of the collectivization of the Russian mind. Finds the book disturbing because it appears that Soviet leaders have succeeded in replacing individual reflection with conditioned reflexes. Concludes that a closer examination shows that the people haven't been broken yet because while they may see no way around the dilemma of total power for the workers or for the bourgeoisie now, they have hope to find a third path some day.

426.  Roberts, Henry L. "Communism: Two Ways of Looking at It." Rev. of *No Third Path. New York Herald Tribune Books* 4 Mar. 1962: 11.

Finds the book "an impressionistic record from within" of the Soviet Union. Sees it is a complex work and describes the central theme as the relationship between the individual and the collective, which, one respondent observed, is what is "changing us all into puppets," not the police. Also deals with Soviet expectations of the final outcome of "peaceful coexistence, China, and recent novels."

427.  "Soviet Sketches." Rev. of *The Future Is Ours, Comrade: Conversations with the Russians. Times Literary Supplement* 3 Feb. 1961: 75.

Briefly describes the genesis of this work, the pseudononymous nature of the author, and the uncertainty of the original language. Claims "it has all the fluency of the best American journalism." Quotes from Irving Levine's preface, and describes the insights into Russian life provided by the conversations with Russians.

# Foreign Language Sources

428. Armand, Monique. "*The Devil Tree* et la linearite." *Trema* 2 (1977): 47-57.

429. Danon-Boileau, L. "L'Abord linguistique des textes litteraires." *Langues Modernes* 78.6 (1984): 477-81.

430. Gault, Pierre, and Monique Armand. "Deconstruction du recit dans *The Painted Bird* de Jerzy Kosinski." *Trema* 1 (1975): 171-89.

431. Genies, Bernard. "Interview with Jerzy Kosinski." *Quinzaine Litteraire* 327 (1980): 6-7. (In French).

432. Gorlier, Claudio. *Approdo Letterario: Rivista Trimestrale di Lettere e Arti* 62 (1973): 136-39.

433. La Polla, Franco. *Un posto nella mente: Il nuovo romanzo Americano: 1962-1982*. Il Portico: Biblioteca di Lettere e Art: Letteratura Straniera 74. Ravenna: Longo, 1983.

434. Matthieussent, Brice. "Mieux qu'un 'best-seller.'"." *Quinzaine Litteraire* 285 (1978): 7.

435. "Ein Nasjon av Videotar: Samtale med Jerzy Kosinski." *Syn og Segn: Norsk Tidsskrift* 89.3 (1983): 134-41.

436. Saalmann, Dieter. "Betrachtungen zur Holokaustliteratur." *Orbis Litterarum: Internation Review of Literary Studies* 36.3 (1981): 243-59.

437. Sugiura, Ginsaku. "Osurubeki Itan no Kansei—Jerzy Kosinski ni tsuite." *Eigo Seinen* 119 (1973): 390-91.

438. Tiefenthaler, Sepp L. "Jerzy Kosinskis dichterische Imagination— Bemerkungen zu seinem Roman *Steps*." *Forms of the American Imagination: Beitrage zur neuren amerikanischen Literatur*. Eds. Sonja Bahn, Arno Heller, Brigitte Scheer-Schazler, and Sepp L. Tiefenthaler. Innsbrucker Beitrage zur Kulturwissenschaft 44. Innsbruck: Instut fur Sprachwissenschaft der Universitat Innsbruck, 1979. 133-45.

439. Tiefenthaler, Sepp L. "Jerzy Kosinski." *Die zeitgenossische amerikanische Roman*. Ed. Gerhard Hoffmann. 3 vols. Munchen: Fink, 1988. 3:214-30.

440. Vallora, Marco. "Televisione secondo Kosinski." *Al-fa-beta* 3 (1981): 22-24.

441. Vree, Freddy de. "Jerzy Kosinski: *Cockpit*, Elckerlyck." *Kunst en Cultuur* 1 Sept. 1975: 26-27.

# Dissertations

442. Bloomfield, Mitchell Bernard. "The Fiction of Jerzy Kosinski: The Perverse in the Modern Imagination." Diss. Michigan State U., 1975.

443. Childress, Ronald. "The Survivor in Jerzy Kosinski's *Cockpit*." Diss. Florida Atlantic U, 1986.

444. Fick, Thomas Hale. "An American Dialectic: Power and Innocence from Cooper to Kosinski." Diss. Indiana U, 1985.

445. Fitzgerald, Sister Ellen. "World War II in the American Novel: Hawkes, Heller, Kosinski, and Vonnegut." Diss. U of Notre Dame, 1974.

446. Golden, Robert Edward. "Violence and Art in Postwar American Literature: A Study of O'Connor, Kosinski, Hawkes, and Pynchon." Diss. U of Rochester, 1972.

447. Granofsky, Ronald. "The Contemporary Symbolic Novel." Diss. Queen's U at Kingston (Canada), 1986.

448. Green, Geoffrey Dennis. "Writers in Exile: Chapters in the Critical Examination of Literature and Society." Diss. State U of New York at Buffalo, 1977.

449. Horowitz, Sara Reva. "Linguistic Displacement in Fictional Responses to the Holocaust: Kosinski, Wiesel, Lind, and Tournier." Diss. Brandeis U, 1985.

450. Hutchinson, James D. "The Art of the Self: The Quest for Authenticity in the novels of Jerzy Kosinski." Diss. U of Denver, 1974.

451. Lipani, David Joseph. "Jerzy Kosinski: A Study of His Novels." Diss. Bowling Green State U, 1973.

452. Raff, Melvin H. "This Above All: The Challenge of Identity in Modern Literature." Diss. U Of Maryland, College Park, 1988.

453. Tepa, Barbara Jane. "Inside the Kaleidoscope: Jerzy Kosinski's Polish and American Contexts." Diss. St. Johns U, 1975.

454. Tiefenthaler, Sepp L. "Jerzy Kosinski: eine Einfuhrung in sein Werk." Diss. U of Innsbruck, 1978.

455. Viscomi, Janice M. "Jerzy Kosinski: Contemporary Novelist as Knight." Diss. U of North Carolina at Chapel Hill, 1986.

456. Vitterite, Nicholas John, Jr. "Descants and Pricksongs as a Modality of Postmodernism: A Study of the Works of Robert Coover and Jerzy Kosinski." Diss. Emory U, 1984.

457. Weinstein, Sharon Rosenbaum. "Comedy and Nightmare: The Fiction of John Hawkes, Kurt Vonnegut, Jr., Jerzy Kosinski, and Ralph Ellison." Diss. U of Utah, 1971.

# Indexes

# Author Index

# Subject Index

**About the Authors**

GLORIA L. CRONIN is Associate Professor of English at Brigham Young University. She is the co-author with Blaine H. Hall of *Saul Bellow: An Annotated Bibliography* and *Jewish American Fiction Writers: An Annotated Bibliography*. She is also co-editor with L. H. Goldman of two collections of essays, *Saul Bellow in the 1980s: A Collection of Critical Essays* and *Mosaic: The Proceedings of the International Saul Bellow Conference, Haifa, Israel*.

BLAINE H. HALL is English Language and Literature Librarian at Brigham Young University. His publications include *Collection Assessment Manual for College and University Libraries*, *Saul Bellow: An Annotated Bibliography*, and *Jewish American Fiction Writers: An Annotated Bibliography*.